DISCARDED

D1518204

The Natural Instability of Markets

The Natural Instability of Markets

Expectations, Increasing Returns, and the Collapse of Capitalism

Michael Perelman

St. Martin's Press
New York

THE NATURAL INSTABILITY OF MARKETS

ISBN 0-312-22121-5

Library of Congress Cataloging-in-Publication Data

Perelman, Michael.
The natural instability of markets : expectations, increasing returns, and the collapse of capitalism / by Michael Perelman.
p. cm.
Includes bibliographical references and index.
ISBN 0-312-22121-5
1. Business cycles. 2. Capitalism. 3. Competition. I. Title.
HB3711.P377 1999
338.5'42—DC21 98-48413
CIP

Design by Letra Libre, Inc.

First edition: June, 1999
10 9 8 7 6 5 4 3 2 1

Contents

Acknowledgments

Several people helped me with this book. First of all, my colleague, Gary Francis, read the manuscript and made a number of helpful suggestions. Judith Klein helped me with the history of business cycle theory. I relied on the expertise of Todd Freeberg of the department of biological sciences of Purdue University to help me avoid errors in understanding the role of biological analogies in economics. Most of all John Legge, of the Graduate School of Management at LaTrobe University in Victoria, Australia painstakingly worked through the manuscript with a fine tooth comb. I owe each of them an enormous debt of gratitude.

I also want to thank the CELT program of California State University, Chico for granting me a semester's leave to complete this book.

PREFACE

The Fragile Foundations of the Triumphant Market

With the collapse of the Soviet Union, capitalism now proudly proclaims its ultimate triumph. Formerly socialist states frantically scramble to remake themselves as market economies. In the United States, everything left of the political center has all but disappeared from the national political dialogue. Markets are supplanting virtually every kind of service that the state previously supplied. Public schools, public prisons, public streets, and even police work are being privatized.

Even so, I am confident that capitalism's victory will be temporary. The market system is so familiar and our institutional memories so short, we tend to forget—even if we knew in the first place—that capitalism is, by its very nature, an inherently unstable system. Today, even World Bank publications admit that financial crises have become more frequent and more severe in recent years (see Caprio and Klingebiel 1997).

Capital has enjoyed moments of triumph before, but they have always been followed by a subsequent disaster. We need to take a step back to recognize just how strange markets are. In a market society, individuals generally do not cooperate directly. Instead, they indirectly coordinate their activities by flashing numbers (prices) to the rest of society. That this system worked at all was a source of amazement to those who watched the market system in its formative years. Adam Smith's metaphor of an invisible hand reflected the almost magical appearance of market forces (Smith 1776, IV.ii.9; 456).

Recurrent depressions and recessions taught many of Smith's successors that the market is not necessarily benign. Over the past few decades, however, this lesson has all but completely worn off. Today, with dangerously few people aware of the breadth of the risks associated with a market economy, we are less prepared than ever to come to grips with a crisis. We have thoughtlessly dismantled much of the regulatory system, which is supposed to contain the risks of crises, along with the welfare system, which was meant to cushion society from the consequences of crises.

With these conditions in mind, the time has come for an analysis of the causes of crises within a market society. This book shows why the force of competition tends to create instability and depression. I am not aware of any other contemporary book that specifically addresses the subject of why markets have an inherent tendency to fall into crises.

This book also takes a fresh look at competition. Nobody before has tried to ask exactly what competition does. This book shows why competition is often not very effective. Competition takes on a significant force only during times of depression and recession. When competition does become strong, it is unselective, destroying fit and unfit alike, while wreaking havoc on society.

This book also suggests that within a market society, we can gain some of the benefits of competition, without adding to the dangers of a depression, by keeping wages high as a means of putting pressure on business. In this way, we do not get the deflationary pressures associated with normal competition. Environmental protection serves the same purpose.

In part, the absence of books that address and consider the natural instability of markets is understandable. The capitalist world has not seen a major depression for more than a half century. In addition, economists are naturally predisposed to find order in the economy. After all, if the economy were absolutely disorderly, they would have nothing to contribute. In addition, the training that economists undergo conditions them to emphasize the tendency of the economy to be stable rather than calling attention to any of the forces that might make for instability.

Finally, economists are a relatively conservative lot. To the extent that they work to justify the status quo, they have strong incentives to portray the economy as stable. If a problem arises, then some outside force, typically the government, is to blame. As Milton Friedman, perhaps the foremost advocate of laissez-faire of the twentieth-century United States, once wrote with embarrassing self-satisfaction, "The fact is that the Great Depression, like most other periods of severe unemployment, was produced by government mismanagement rather than by inherent instability of the private economy" (Friedman 1962: 38).

For Friedman, as for most economists today, markets are natural. Markets have natural rates of unemployment and natural rates of interest. Anything that interferes with the free functioning of markets is unnatural, if not downright perverse. In truth, markets are not natural any more than they are stable. In this book, I will make the case that markets would be even more unstable than they are if it were not for the inertia created by laws and customs that supposedly impede markets.

Despite the best efforts of economists, most people intuitively realize that the economy is not stable. I suspect that few people feel a need for economists to tell them why the economy is stable. They are not interested in economists' fixed-point theorems and the other parts of the mathematical apparatus of economic stability theory. Instead, rightly or wrongly, people often look to economists for predictions that can prepare them for unexpected changes in the economy. They are more concerned about the possibility of a reversal in the stock market or a disorder that might cost them their job.

In fact, when people learn that I am an economist, more often than not, the first question they ask me is, "will the stock market go up or down?" Little, if anything, in our training as economists equips us to predict the future course of the economy. In all modesty, when asked if the stock market will go up or down, I can confidently answer "yes." Of course, I am certain that it will go up. I am equally sure that it will go down. I do not know which will happen first. I do not know by how much or when it will go down or up, but it will move.

I am far from alone in my ignorance about the future. Nobody else has accurate information about the future. We can only make educated guesses about what is in store for us. Unfortunately, in our educated guesses, most of us, economists included, overestimate our education and underestimate the degree to which we guess.

If we have to rely on guess-work, we have a good reason to predict stability. Suppose that economies crash about once every thirty years. On any given day, the economy will stand a chance of less than one in ten thousand of crashing. If I am concerned about my reputation for accuracy, if someone asks me if the economy will crash tomorrow, I would be well advised not to stick my neck out to predict such an unlikely event. If I am wrong, I will look foolish.

If I proclaim that nothing will happen tomorrow, I will probably be proven to be correct. If a crash should occur, my reputation will still be relatively untarnished, since I know that just about all of my colleagues will be wrong as well.

Just as geologists know full well that San Francisco will eventually experience an earthquake, I know that the economy will again suffer another severe depression. So, now the time has come to discuss why the economy is unstable, as well as the surprising source of the relative stability that we do enjoy. In the process, we will also take note of the analysis of those few economists who have glimpsed the nature of this instability. So, buckle up and enjoy the ride.

Chapter 1 of this book discusses the way that economists work, especially emphasizing their zeal in creating models that are supposed to prove that the economy is always in or near an equilibrium. This chapter is intended to show why economists are ill prepared to confront the instability that is inherent in markets. Chapter 2 concerns the way in which that abstract, imaginary world in which most economists work functions. Chapter 3 describes how economists introduced the concept of business cycles as a way to minimize the role of economic crises. By treating the boom-and-bust pattern of the economy as a periodic function, economic crises seemed to be less threatening. Eventually, even the concept of business cycles seemed to raise too many questions about the functioning of markets. As a result, economists began to treat them as illusions, arguing that the economy is always near an equilibrium. Chapter 4 discusses two economists, John Maynard Keynes and Joseph Alois Schumpeter, who did acknowledge the instability of markets. This chapter also describes how their self-described disciples managed to wring the analysis of instability out of their theories. Chapter 5 begins the heart of the book by reconsidering the nature of the competitive process. I find many similarities between my understanding of competition and Stephen J. Gould's theory of punctuated equilibrium.

Chapter 6 extends the analysis of competition by making the case that competitive markets tend to fall into depressions, unless some external support is available. This support may come from anticompetitive practices, as well as from monetary or fiscal policies. Chapter 7 describes methods of simulating competition through high wages or environmental controls. Simulated competition provides the benefits of competition proper, without the dangerous deflationary pressures associated with ordinary market competition. Chapter 8 presents a thumbnail sketch of the history of competition in the United States. Chapter 9 concerns the role of inertia in stabilizing the economy. Finally, Chapter 10 ties up some loose threads.

A Warning

In calling for a different understanding of the nature of markets, I do not pretend to be some visionary economic soothsayer who has discovered the loadstone that has eluded all previous economists. Like every other reasonable scholar, I know that virtually everything found in this book has precedents elsewhere.

I have drawn upon conventional economists from the nineteenth century, radicals, conservatives, and Keynesians, as well as from my peers. I have also found a great deal of resonance in the work of the paleontologist Stephen J. Gould. Each approach has something to offer in understanding the economy; none has a monopoly on the truth.

I am aware that hard and fast truths, over and above some commonsense propositions, are nonexistent in economics. Evidence and proofs that we once convincingly brandished will soon fall out of fashion as some future turn of events reveals a flaw in the theory. Books and articles, which once commanded enormous respect, will soon appear foolish.

But fads come and fads go. In a few more years, after events cast the newest ideas into doubt, people will come forth with some alternative theories. In the process, they are likely to rediscover some of these now-rejected articles, proud to have found antecedents for their new theory in a forgotten corner of our world.

I am also aware that no book is ever complete. In what follows, I will make some strong, even heretical statements, knowing full well that some parts will some need revision in the future. Either I or another person could probably write an entire volume expanding upon the implications of any one of a number of these individual claims. Such a book could end up by qualifying parts of my original notions, explaining away seemingly inconsistent examples and mustering still more evidence to support the essential idea.

In the process, I, or any other author for that matter, would make still more claims, many of which would require still another volume to amplify them more fully. In the meantime, I might be more than ready to modify my original thesis, now knowing more than I did when I began the whole process.

An exasperated Harry Truman, tired of economists explaining their theories with "on the one hand" and "on the other hand," is said to have cried out that he was looking for a one-handed economist. In truth, President Truman gave the profession too much credit. One-handed economists are in the majority.

For the most part, subtleties elude those of us who have undergone training as economists. We tend to write in absolutes. In our eyes, single causes explain major events; with broad strokes, we confidently proclaim some absolute truth: Perhaps that everything either tends to converge or perhaps everything becomes very different, all the while ignoring any number of exceptions or extenuating situations.

Having made my peace, I will now proceed to the story. Well, not quite. First, I will digress and consider the nature of economic analysis, to find out why economists have overlooked the tendencies that form the central focus of this book.

The Natural Instability of Markets

CHAPTER 1

How Economists Work: A Prelude to the Main Theme of This Book

What Is Instability?

This book concerns the instability inherent in market economies. I will discuss why markets are unstable and why the relative stability that we do enjoy comes from outside of the abstract relations of markets. Let me confess at the outset that I do not have a good definition of economic instability. Instead, I will follow the practice of the Supreme Court of the United States, which avoided the necessity of defining pornography by assuming that everybody knew it when they saw it.

We associate economic instability with a steep drop in the economy, but rapid declines in the economy do not necessarily indicate instability. For example, every January, following the intense Christmas buying period, the U.S. economy experiences a sharp fall in economic activity that most economists consider to be normal.

Most people think of the Great Depression as our most recent experience with massive instability, although the fall in economic activity in 1980 was as sharp. Once this latter decline reversed itself, this incident was largely forgotten, except by the relatively small number of people who never recovered. Although the massive stock sell-off of 1987 was as dramatic as the crash of 1929, because the market recovered soon thereafter, people now regard that event as a healthy correction.

In short, instability is to some extent subjective. At any time in the economy, some people make bad decisions; others fall victim to bad luck.

Even during a general boom, isolated geographic regions may experience hard times. Such events do not constitute instability.

Similarly, few people perceive exceptionally good times as evidence of instability. A raging bull market on Wall Street seems to be the normal state of affairs. Only later, in a booming market, do we hear some pundits express concern that the bubble may burst.

I guess that we can say that society subjectively perceives economic instability once people across the economy tend to automatically think of another person's woes as part of a larger economic problem rather than bad luck, poor decisions, or the normal sort of reverses typical of a region or an industry in decline.

The Three Worlds of Economic Knowledge

If you are already familiar with the way that economics has become an increasingly abstract discipline, distant from the real economic lives of the masses of people, you may already be conversant with some of the material in this first section. Now let us return to the idea of instability.

Although instability is a central feature of a market economy, conventional economic theory is poorly suited to analyzing this subject. An economist is able to predict some things fairly accurately, as long as conditions do not change very much, in the same sense that a lazy weather forecaster could do a fair job by predicting that tomorrow's weather will be pretty much like today's.

The lazy weather forecaster cannot do me much good. I know that the weather will not remain unchanged for long. I want to be able to know how to prepare for sudden changes in the weather. I want to know how likely a rain shower is today.

The methods that economists use to predict the economy are to some extent similar to the technique of our hypothetical weather forecaster. We assume that a few things can change, but by and large, we expect that the overall situation will be fairly stable. Large changes will definitely occur, but having no idea of when they will, the forecaster merely assumes a large degree of stability.

The same principles apply in the economy. Nobody has access to the information required to make accurate predictions. We can only make educated guesses. As I mentioned earlier, in our educated guesses, most of us, economists included, overestimate our education and underestimate the degree to which we guess.

Yet we desperately crave the illusion of certainty that a seemingly scientific forecast offers. Kenneth Arrow, a Nobel Prize-winning economist, likes to tell a tale to illustrate this point. During the Second World War, he was an Air Force weather forecaster. The military assigned some officers the task of forecasting the weather a month ahead. His statisticians calculated that these forecasts were no better than numbers pulled out of a hat. The forecasters agreed and asked their superiors to relieve them of this duty. The reply was: "The Commanding General is well aware that the forecasts are no good. However, he needs them for planning purposes" (Arrow 1992: 46–47).

Arrow concluded, "Vast ills have followed a belief in certainty, whether historical inevitability, grand diplomatic designs, or extreme views on economic policy. When developing policy with wide effects for an individual or society, caution is needed because we cannot predict the consequences" (Arrow 1992: 46).

Although economic predictions may be of questionable value, some understanding of a few basic principles of economics is useful for understanding the economy. The depth of this understanding, however, is rather shallow. Consider the testimony of Herbert Stein, who was the chief economic adviser to the Nixon administration. According to Stein, "It may seem a shocking thing to say, but most of the economics that is usable for advising on public policy is at about the level of the introductory undergraduate course" (Stein 1991: 6). Alain Enthoven, who was chief economist of the Department of Defense during the early 1960s and later one of the gurus of managed health care, came to a similar conclusion. He explained to his audience at the annual meeting of the American Economic Association:

> [T]he tools of analysis that we use [at the Defense Department] are the simplest, most fundamental concepts of economic theory, combined with the simplest quantitative methods. The requirements for success in this line of work are a thorough understanding of and, if you like, belief in the relevance of such concepts as marginal products and marginal costs. . . .
>
> The economic theory that we are using (in the department) is the theory that most of us learned as sophomores. The reason Ph.D's are required is that many economists do not believe what they have learned until they have gone through graduate school and acquired a vested interest (in conventional economic theory). (Enthoven 1963: 422)

We should not be surprised that those economists, whose work consists of simple "back of the envelope" calculations, constitute the smallest and perhaps least influential group within the economics profession. The simplicity of their techniques is deceptive. In fact, they are often the most skillful practitioners of the craft. Even so, the simplicity of their techniques has one serious drawback. The seemingly off-hand nature of their calculations suggests that anybody could qualify as an economist—an impression that would hardly appeal to members of a profession who have devoted five or ten years to their postgraduate education.

Imagine yourself to be the vice president in charge of planning for a multinational corporation. If you were to base a decision on the work of back-of-the-envelope economists and your project turned out to be disastrous, your job and your reputation could be in jeopardy. In retrospect, the seemingly simple calculations of one of these economists might appear to have little more basis than a hunch. If, instead, you relied on a very expensive pseudoscientific computer-based model, your mistake might possibly be easier to explain away.

So, the cost and expense of a complicated economic model might appear to be justified as a relatively cheap insurance policy with which you might be able to cover a part of your derrière in the event of a mishap. As John Maynard Keynes noted, "Worldly wisdom teaches that it is better for reputation to fail conventionally than to succeed unconventionally" (Keynes 1936: 158). For all these reasons, and perhaps because of the difficulty of doing this work well, the economists that inhabit this world make up only a tiny proportion of the profession.

The second world of economics is ideological. Economists as a group are highly conservative. More often than not, they project an emotional commitment to the principles of the market. The ideological economist is less interested in predicting the future or even explaining the past than in justifying a particular ideological point of view. In this respect, economic theory becomes, in the words of Piero Sraffa, a scathing critic of abstract economics, "essentially a pedagogic instrument, somewhat like the study of the classics, and, unlike the study of the exact sciences and law, its purposes are exclusively those of training the mind" (Sraffa 1926: 535).

The third world of economics is the world of science. This world is imaginary, but it nonetheless exercises a great power over economists. Many economists are absolutely convinced that they live in this nonexistent world.

For more than a century, academic economists have been trying to elevate the study of the market to the status of a science. This venture serves two overlapping purposes. To begin with, to the extent that economists can convince the world that their theories are grounded in science, they can win respect. In addition, if economics is a science, then noneconomists, people who supposedly lack the proper scientific credentials to participate in economic debates, would have to defer to professional economists.

Membership in this group of economists by no means excludes an ideological commitment. In fact, many ideological economists are dual citizens of the world of science.

Most people initially come to the study of economics out of a sincere desire to learn about how the economy works. None of these three worlds offers them much support. The first world, the people who inhabit the world of the policy makers, generally accepts the status quo. Their mindset is often one that makes them unable to see the forest because of the preoccupation with a few specific trees.

In Europe, where individual economies are smaller, the premium on the understanding of trees is higher. For that reason, in Europe, economists who inhabit the world of economic policy enjoy more prestige than they do in the United States. In many of these countries, such as England, France, Germany, Portugal, Norway, and Greece, economists of this stripe have occupied the highest political office in the country (Frey and Eichenberger 1992: 216).

The people who inhabit the ideological world have even less to offer, but in their fervor, they often win over converts who mistakenly confuse the certainty that comes from a firmly held ideology with objective analysis.

The would-be scientifically inclined economists probably do the most damage. They presently control virtually all the major economics departments in the United States and increasingly are expanding their influence abroad. Once graduate students enter one of these programs, they must devote most of their energies to the study of mathematical and statistical tools. In the end, few students end up with the time or the inclination to wrestle with problems in a realistic way (see Perelman 1996, Ch. 1).

Finally, let me note that none of these three worlds offer much help in understanding the basic instability that pervades a market economy.

Economics as a Science

Let us turn to the subject of economics as a science again. Thomas Kuhn, perhaps the most influential historian of science, once ironically remarked, "It may, for example, be significant that economists argue less about whether their field is a science than do practitioners of some other fields of social science. Is that because economists know what science is? (Kuhn 1962: 161).

Kuhn, a historian of science who was sympathetic to economics as a discipline, suggested that the reason economists could present their discipline as a science was that they fundamentally agreed on the core of their analysis.

Despite economists' fervent wish to be as scientific as physicists, our discipline is considerably different from physics, the science that economists typically take to be the quintessential science. We can find stark evidence of the gap between the respective ways of economists and physicists in a report on a conference between leading representatives of the two disciplines. The physicists were amazed at how mathematically sophisticated economists were. The economists, in turn, were shocked at the physicists' lack of rigor. The economists thought that science meant mathematical proofs of theories and statistical tests. In contrast, the physicists spend most of their time trying to explain phenomena. In this endeavor, the physicists would just follow their noses or use computer simulations to test ideas, without too much regard for abstract theory (Pool 1989: 701).

The reporter who brought this conference to the attention of the outside world attributed some of the differences in the respective cultures of economists and physicists to the lack of economic data. Indeed, precision is a hallmark of science. Physical scientists can measure almost everything with increasing exactitude.

In physics, as measurement becomes extended down to the nanosphere, physicists raise questions about their science far faster than they can answer them. Even so, while facing the fact that Newtonian physics is painfully incomplete, physicists can still verify their theories to some degree with experiments. In addition, even if they cannot be certain about the ultimate truth of their theories, physicists can congratulate themselves in their victories that manifest themselves in the wonders of high technology.

Economists live in a far more unsettling world. Their theories, except for a few commonsensical truisms, remain forever a matter of conjecture. Economists still debate the causes of events that occurred centuries ago. The prospects of nearing a resolution on such matters seems as distant as ever. John Maynard Keynes, perhaps the most outstanding economist of the twentieth century, once recalled:

> Professor Planck, of Berlin, the famous originator of the Quantum Theory, once remarked to me that in his early life he had thought of studying economics, but had found it too difficult! Professor Planck could easily master the whole corpus of mathematical economics in a few days. He did not mean that! But the amalgam of logic and intuition and the wide knowledge of facts, most of which are not precise, which is required for economic interpretation in its highest form is, quite truly, overwhelmingly difficult for

> those whose gift mainly consists in the power to imagine and pursue to their furthest points the implications and prior conditions of comparatively simple facts which are known with a high degree of precision. (Keynes 1924: 186)

Planck seems to have realized that economics is difficult or, to be more accurate impossible, in the sense that scientific analysis of the economy is impossible. Economic activity depends on the behavior of millions and even billions of people. Economists have no way of comprehending the entirety of the complicated structure of an actual economy.

To bring the complexity of economic activity down to manageable proportions, economists impose stark assumptions about reality and then construct mathematical models of what they assume to be the main features of the economy. In fact, economists actually rely on such models to communicate with each other. Time and again, I have tried to explain an idea to a fellow economist, only to hear the demand that I first put my idea in the context of a mathematical model. As Paul Krugman once observed, "Since economics . . . is strongly oriented toward mathematical models, any economic argument that has not been expressed in that form tends to remain invisible" (Krugman 1990: 3).

Economic models are generally nothing more than an amalgam of highly complex mathematics, built around simplistic assumptions about the way the people behave. For example, economic models generally unrealistically assume that all people are purely rational, profit-maximizing creatures.

Most of these economic models merely tell the story of people or firms that are trying to maximize their income or profit. The end of the story is almost invariably supposed to show how economic incentives invariably lead the model to a stable equilibrium, perhaps with a few minor modifications, such as a change in monetary or fiscal polity. Economists give the most prestige to those whose models use the most sophisticated mathematical techniques, even though most of these stories could easily be told in a simple, even commonsensical fashion.

Once a model is completed, economists are permitted to append a short section that discusses the implications of the model. Some discussions are very modest, noting that the model corroborates or calls into question some earlier models. From time to time, the conclusion contains speculation that goes well beyond the narrow framework of the model. Since the speculative ruminations are unsupported, their only effect may be to suggest a new research project for another economist.

Evaluating Models

Economic models supposedly serve a purpose in weeding out ideas that are contradictory. Given the restricted nature of economic models, you might expect that economists would find general agreement among themselves. For the most part, they do. Indeed, several surveys have documented a far-reaching consensus among professional economists about a number of basic questions (Frey, Pomerehne, Schneider, and Gilbert 1984; Jackstadt, Huskey, Marx, and Hill 1990).

The idea of agreement among economists might seem surprising to an outsider. Economists are forever bickering among each other. An uninitiated person wandering too near a pack of economists may be surprised to find many of these highly trained professionals snarling at each other. Albert Hirschman, one of the most reflective of all modern economists, observed that the disputatious nature of economists "suggests an interesting point about the scientific status of economics." In the sciences, joint Nobel Prizes are given to collaborators, where in economics, the prize is sometimes split between two persons who have worked to disprove the other's work (Hirschman 1981: 8).

The explanation of the seemingly contradictory observations about the extent of agreement among economists is fairly simple. Economists generally share a basic vision about the nature of the workings of markets. Like warring religious sects, they strongly differ about minor details.

How could economists come to a resolution about their various theories? Consider what happens if I find data that seem to refute my model and suggest that your interpretation of the situation might be correct. If I am a clever economist, I will set out to rehabilitate my model by making slight changes in assumptions or by adjusting the data to avoid the need to reject my preconceived theory (see Reder 1982).

This sort of behavior might seem to violate the basic norms of scientific research, but economics differs from science in that economic data are, for the most part, notoriously imprecise (Morgenstern 1963). To cope with the deficiencies of their data, economists have developed a wide array of techniques to massage their data, increasing some numbers and decreasing others, supposedly to make them more realistic. Unfortunately, we have no real standard to determine which sort of adjustment of the data is appropriate. As a result, the data become more or less arbitrary.

Not only is the quality of the data poor, but the highly sophisticated statistical techniques that economists use are very fragile, in the sense that they are often extremely sensitive to minor variations in the data. Moreover, an only slightly different statistical technique can give dramatically different results. In addition, with small changes in an admittedly unrealistic assumption about the underlying model, the same data can give contradictory conclusions.

Consequently, these exercises produce highly inconclusive results that rarely, if ever, change anybody's mind. So, unlike physics, where new experimental data raise previously unimaginable possibilities, economic questions are perennial, revolving around seemingly theological disputes about human cognition and behavior or the speed at which markets adjust.

As a result, economists find themselves still debating the causes of events that occurred hundreds of years ago. In the end, economists just select those studies that reinforce their prior beliefs, while pointing out the limits of the studies that might conflict with those beliefs. In the process, economists become passionately attached to minor variations of the assumptions in their models, giving the impression of a jumble of conflicting ideas.

Let's Get Real

The bitter disputes that divide most economists seem to concern minor modifications of an abstract model. In reality, what generally divides economists are a few simple questions about the nature of human behavior and how fast an economy will respond to a given stimulus. As for the first question, nobody has ever found a satisfactory way to come to grips with human nature. Even though we should be able to get a handle on the second question, economists have come no closer to reaching a consensus about this subject during the last century.

I would add that most economists are too emotionally wedded to their belief that market societies are the best of all possible worlds. As a result, they resist delving into anything that might call market organization into question. Those who dare to raise troubling questions will face serious sanctions. Younger economists will find jobs hard to get and to keep. More established economists will find difficulty in getting their work published in professional journals.

To make matters worse, few economists have a good feel for history—either the history of the economy or a history of their discipline. As a result, they take whatever exists at the moment as natural and even permanent, even though, at another level, they realize that the world is rapidly changing. Perhaps what is most dangerous of all about the economic way of thinking is that economists force what they do know about the economy into an abstract framework that bears no resemblance to reality, then bury it within a mountain of unnecessary mathematical sophistication.

With some prodding, any honest economist can tell you what is wrong with economics. We desperately want our discipline to be scientific, so much that we distort what we do. As a result, we end up with something that is neither scientific nor particularly relevant to understanding the economy.

I do not mean to say that we do not know anything about the economy. Of course, we do. Unfortunately, as a result of the emphasis on abstract modeling, most economists know precious little about the actual operation of the economy: how businesspeople make decisions, how work is organized on the factory floor, what makes people want to contribute to an organization, or how new ideas evolve.

In the end, we eliminate from economic theory everything that makes an economy dynamic. As a result, we make ourselves hopelessly incapable of confronting the nature of economic instability.

Dynamic Economies and Stable Models

In their zeal to discover laudable qualities in a market economy, most economists credit market societies with two somewhat contradictory qualities: stability and dynamism. Not entirely without reason, most economists regard capitalism as the most dynamic system of economic organization that could ever be devised. True, they often fail to comment that some of this dynamism reflects an ability to extract wealth parasitically from less powerful nations and a willingness to exploit the environment with abandon. Even so, the technical dynamism of modern market societies has been remarkable.

This discussion of dynamism usually takes place as an informal commentary on market societies in general. In their formal models, economists usually assume at best a more restricted form of dynamism. There, they postulate that all parties do behave dynamically, reacting almost instantaneously to any opportunity for profit, but in these models the quick reactions merely return the economy to a position of stability. Pick up almost any book that praises the economics of markets. You will see something there about how quickly markets adjust. No matter the cause—a crop failure, a new technology, or changing tastes—markets supposedly respond expeditiously toward a new but stable equilibrium.

This sort of dynamism is useful in trying to prove stability, but a healthy economy does not have a stable equilibrium. As Joseph Schumpeter, whom

I will discuss in more detail later, insisted, "Whereas a stationary feudal economy would still be a feudal economy, and a stationary socialist economy would still be a socialist economy, stationary capitalism is a contradiction in terms" (Schumpeter 1943: 174).

Schumpeter located economic upheavals in the creation of new technologies rather than an upswell of competitive forces. He insisted that instead of smoothly approaching an equilibrium, a dynamic economy destroys entire industries while it creates brand-new sectors (Schumpeter 1950). His prime example was the reconstruction of the economy around the railroad. For Schumpeter, "Railroadization is our standard example by which to illustrate the working of our model. . . . [Many factors] combine to make the essential features of our evolutionary process more obvious in this than they are in any other case. More easily than in any other can the usual objections to our analysis be silenced by a simple reference to obvious facts" (Schumpeter 1939: 304).

Alas, Schumpeter remains an exception. Few modern economists other than Schumpeter understood how unstable the real economy is.

CHAPTER 2

The Imaginary World of Economic Equilibrium and Stability

The Blinders of Equilibrium Theory

I cannot repeat enough my concern that economists rely on overly simple models. The more complex the subject, the more extreme the simplification becomes. The most complex subject in economics is what economists call "general equilibrium theory"—the study of how an economy as a whole arrives at an equilibrium.

The formal study of general equilibrium began with the work of Leon Walras (1874). Although Walras used a highly simplified model to represent the complexities of the economy, he hoped that a knowledge of the nature of equilibrium would indirectly contribute to our understanding of how a real economy works.

In his words: "the conclusions of pure science bring us to the very threshold of applied science" (Walras 1874: 255). Walras believed that "it did not matter whether or not we observed [free competition] in the real world since, strictly speaking, it was sufficient that we should be able to form a conception of it" (Walras 1874: 255).

Walras applied this same philosophy to the study of crises. Toward the end of his book, *Elements of Pure Economics,* he explained: "For just as a lake is, at times, stirred to its very depths by a storm, so also the market is sometimes thrown into violent confusion by *crises,* which are sudden and general disturbances of equilibrium. The more we know of the ideal conditions of equilibrium, the better we shall be able to control or prevent these crises" (Walras 1874: 380–1).

While we can applaud Walras' hope of ultimately learning to understand instability, his work is of little value in this regard. His analysis of the still lake does nothing to reveal the nature of instability. For the most part, Walras' successors enthusiastically took up his mantle in studying equilibrium, but they showed no interest whatsoever in looking beyond the world of still lakes into the question of instability.

Let us consider the nature of equilibria for a moment. Keynes' most famous words, "In the long run, we are all dead," returned to the water metaphor. Popular writers, and even economists who should know better, often quote this expression to recommend a general attitude of nonchalance about the future. Keynes' context suggests a far narrower concern.

In truth, Keynes seemed to have something entirely different in mind. His next sentence read: "Economists set themselves too easy, too useless a task if in tempestuous seasons they can only tell us that when the storm is long past the ocean is flat again" (Keynes 1923a: 65). Specifically, Keynes was taking on the economists' tendency to avoid analyzing difficult problems by assuming that in the long run, the economy will reach a stable equilibrium.

To make matters worse, economists then convince themselves that these abstract models hold the key to solving real-world problems. Keynes himself complained, "Many people are trying to solve the problem of unemployment with a theory which is based on the assumption that there is no unemployment" (Keynes 1933: 350).

Rather than conjecture about long-run tendencies to attain equilibria, Keynes contended that economists must learn to deal with short-run instability. Keynes' warning soon bore bitter fruit. Only six years after Keynes wrote about the certainty of death in the long run, the upheaval of the Great Depression reminded the world just how unstable market economies can be.

In the long run, that depression eventually subsided, but not until more than a decade had passed. Could anyone seriously console another person whose life had been thrown into shambles by a serious depression with a comment to the effect that the economic downturn would only be a short-run affair of a decade or so?

Even so, economists still insist on training their students with theorems and anecdotes that supposedly demonstrate that whenever anything knocks the economy off kilter, the system tends to return to an equilibrium. Walras' original intention has been long forgotten.

Equilibrium Models within Dynamic Economies

Economists borrowed the notion of an equilibrium from engineering, where it means a balancing of forces so that the system remains at rest.

Within this framework, nothing within the economy moves the system out of equilibrium. Only some outside force can move the system away from the equilibrium.

An engineer designing a bridge would find the concept of an equilibrium useful, but what value would it have to an economist trying to study the unruly behavior of an economy? We can assume the existence of all the equilibria that we want; our task as economists must be to understand the real world of change, rather than dream up a hypothetical economy at rest.

We need to discover what makes an economy break out of an equilibrium either to grow or to collapse. In this regard, we have not made much progress. To this day, economists have not come up with an analysis of the Great Depression that is satisfactory to a majority of economists.

Besides, if the economy is so dynamic, why should we think of it as always moving toward an equilibrium? Following in the tradition of Keynes and Walras, let me use still another water analogy. Suppose that I walk across a room carrying a glass of water. If you look closely, you can see the water sloshing back and forth on the walls of the glass. If I am not too exuberant, none of the water will spill, because gravitational forces will pull the water back into the glass. Water, as Keynes noted, seeks its own level—an equilibrium. So, my dynamism—walking across the room—is not at all incompatible with the concept of an equilibrium.

But now we come to the problem: just how relevant is the concept of equilibrium to my little venture across the room. If we want to talk about my dynamism, the gravitational force of the water seems peripheral to the story. The force is still there, but we might want to pay closer attention to what makes me change my location in the first place. You might be interested to know that I see a friend at the other side of the room, motivating me to walk. Or you might want to learn about how I use my muscles to put my body in motion, but the forces that keep the water from spilling out of my glass, in this case, would not be a major concern.

If I become too animated and let the water spill out onto an innocent bystander, the errant water may suddenly grab our attention. In that case, we would more interested in the disequilibrium of the water rather than the tendency to an equilibrium. The wayward water might cause me to interrupt my trip across the room. Of course, if I became too distracted, I might not even have noticed the accident.

We might also need to take into account that the water has some inertia. Even so, concentrating on the equilibrium forces of the water seems to be inappropriate to understanding the dynamism of my trip.

Now let us move back from the story of the trip across the room to the economy. We want to understand what forces make economies grow and develop, but growth and development create disequilibria. These forces do not just spill a little water; they destroy entire industries and displace untold numbers of workers. This line of thought so far should be very familiar to anyone even remotely acquainted with the work of Schumpeter, who taught that if we concentrate all of our attention on the forces of equilibrium, we will lose sight of the sources of dynamism in the economy.

Unfortunately, with rare exceptions, economists have done just that—they emphasize the forces that lead to equilibrium. In fact, economists tend to regard any idea that cannot be put into a mathematical model of equilibrium as beyond the pale of legitimate economic reasoning. To make matters worse, economists narrow their vision even further. In their models, the only acceptable force that can possibly keep an economy on course is profit-maximizing behavior.

We have seen that the dynamic forces in the economy do not just impel us along the road of progress. They also lead to upheavals, which can and do cause incalculable devastation, and even threaten the very destruction of the economy. I intend to describe how other factors that limit the dynamism of the economy are indispensable to preventing an economy from self-destructing.

Price Stability and the Economy

Given their penchant for explaining away any hint of instability, most economists comfortingly depict the natural functioning of the price system in terms of the economy gracefully approaching a state of blissful equilibrium. According to conventional economic theory, once money enters into common use and markets spread, arbitrary prices should begin to give way to market prices. In the long run, market forces should cause local prices to tend to equalize across entire economies, except for differences in transportation costs.

Important questions still remain. Will these prices be stable? Or even more important, why should we believe that these prices guide the economy along a stable path? Economists generally avoid such questions. Instead, they offer up a theory of a long-run tendency toward an equilibrium state, but this theory generally assumes away any of the forces that could lead the economy to instability.

Yet, price stability is crucial within the framework of conventional economics. Here is the explanation of Dennis Robertson:

> But in fact any violent or prolonged exhibition of instability in the value of money affects not only the distribution but also the creation of wealth; for it threatens to undermine the basis of contract and business expectation on which our economic order is built up. That order is largely based upon the institution of contract—on the fact, that is, that people enter into binding agreements with one another to perform certain actions at a future date, for remuneration which is fixed here and now in terms of money. A violent or prolonged change in the value of money saps the confidence with which people accept or make undertakings of this nature. (Robertson 1928: 13)

Many economists regard prices as a form of information that supposedly guides economic behavior. As Robertson noted, if businesspeople cannot trust this information, they will be hesitant to enter into long term contracts, which are essential to the functioning of a modern economy.

The question remains: Why should we expect prices to be stable? Most economists never bother to address that question. Instead, they usually content themselves with extending the assumption of a tendency toward an equilibrium to a belief that prices will be relatively stable in the absence of any interference by the government or monetary authorities.

Of course, prices should not be absolutely rigid. Consider the rapid decline in computer prices over the last few decades. If these prices had been stable—that is, if they had not declined—the vigorous growth of the demand for computers would have been far less spectacular. Too few resources would have found their way to the computer industry, creating a substantial inefficiency.

In short, prices should be flexible enough adapt to new technologies or the development of new patterns of demand. However, both of these factors are relatively stable. In this spirit, I will refer to stable prices as prices that accurately track the underlying structure of demand and technology.

A market economy should be able to function relatively well, even if prices do not exactly match the ideal prices. Common sense suggests that the greater the mismatch, the worse the economy should be expected to perform; however, the possibility remains that even a small error in prices could create enormous negative consequences (Lancaster and Lipsey 1956). Economic theory cannot give us any conclusive answers in this regard, but most economists would guess that a small degree of price instability would create less error than a regime of wild price instability.

History suggests that the economy often can absorb a certain degree of price instability without any great mishap. However, if prices become too unstable, economic agents will be unable to distinguish the information that prices are supposed to provide from the noise in the price structure. Within this context, both too much and too little price stability can threaten the health of the economy.

Stability and Delayed Marketization

If markets are inherently unstable, why don't we see evidence of this instability every day? To understand the reason for the semblance of stability, keep in mind that the process of marketization remains incomplete.

Markets date back at least thousands of years. Keynes once identified capitalism as a "Babylonian Economy," observing that ancient clay tablets provide "details of business from far back—from the Babylonian period" so that "now for the first time we can view economic history in a long perspective. . . . We learn that many of the practices most characteristic of private capitalism were already highly developed in certain parts of the world four thousand years ago" (O'Donnell 1992: 812).

In Babylonia, as in the rest of the ancient world where markets existed they were but a minor part of the economy. For example, when the Spartans warned Cyrus the Great not to harm any city of Greece, Cyrus sarcastically responded: "I have never yet been afraid of any men, who have a set place in the middle of their city, where they come together to cheat each other and forswear themselves" (Herodotus 1942, Bk. 1, Ch. 153). The Greek historian Herodotus commented: "Cyrus intended these words as a reproach against all the Greeks, because of their having market-places where they buy and sell which is a custom unknown to the Persians, who never make purchases in open marts, and indeed have not in their whole country a single marketplace" (Bk. 1, Ch. 153).

Although a number of economic historians now see markets pervading even ancient societies, in Athens and elsewhere, the practice of barter limited the extent of markets. Moreover, in early times, barter was not a strictly economic calculation. Even when goods were sold on the market, custom and tradition remained an important component of price (see Dalton 1982).

Sometimes these customs required that specific commodities exchange for one another in fixed proportions (See Marx 1977: 182; Mandel 1970: i: 73ff; Polanyi 1957; and Oppenheim 1957). As John Stuart Mill observed, in areas where competition has not yet taken hold, "The habitual regulator is customs, modified from time to time by notions existing in the minds of purchasers and sellers, of some kind of equity or justice" (Mill 1848: 243). Since custom varied from place to place, these prices were largely local.

While a rule that a bride was worth four oxen might seem irrational to us today, these fixed-price rules were necessary as an initial basis for an orderly economy. In Marx's words, these traditional "prices" were "indispensable [in providing] social stability and independence from mere chance and arbitrariness" at the time (Marx 1967, 3: 793). Later, as market relations took on more importance relative to custom and tradition, producers began to compare the advantages of producing goods for themselves relative to selling a good on the market in order to purchase from another person (3: 793). Even so, prices did not adjust immediately: "[The] greater part of all . . . commodities, especially at the less developed stages of . . . society, will continue to be estimated in terms of the former measure of value, which has now become antiquated and illusory" (Marx 1977: 214).

The clumsiness of barter created a need for a particular commodity, money, to be used as a measure of exchange. At first, the standard monetary unit was a head of livestock (Marx 1977: 183; see also Einzig 1966, chs. 5, 6, 10, 13, and 16). The word capitalism is related to a head of cattle.

Early coins were apparently denominated in terms of livestock units (Einzig 1966; see also Marx 1849–51: 197). The Latin word pecunia, as well as the English term fee, and the Indian word rupee all have etymological roots referring to livestock (Einzig 1966; but see Keynes 1920–1926: 258; see also Marx 1977: 193).

The introduction of money facilitated the development of capitalism and provided the edifice upon which capitalism eventually stood. Capitalism, in turn, led to the disintegration of most of the traditional customs and institutions.

Karl Marx and Frederick Engels exaggerated a bit in the famous phrase of the *Communist Manifesto,* "All that is solid melts into air" (Marx and Engels 1848: 111). A few vestiges of these traditional customs and institutions managed to survive. Some of them have provided invaluable inertia that has steadied the market and prevented more frequent and more threatening crises.

Faith and Credit

Money, even paper money, still lacked the flexibility required to allow a modern capitalist society to take hold. For a truly dynamic economy to emerge, credit was required. The state of the credit system is probably the most mysterious of all general economic conditions. Today, credit is so familiar that we take it for granted—at least so long as the economy remains relatively stable.

In earlier times, when it was still novel, people recognized how wondrous credit really is. Consider for a moment, the joy of William Paterson on obtaining the charter of the Bank of England in 1694, using the money he had won in privateering. He exclaimed: "The bank hath benefit of all the interest on all moneys which it creates out of nothing" (cited in Quigley 1966: 49).

The bankers were not the only winners in such ventures. John Peyton, a southerner, while visiting Chicago in 1848, learned how vehemently people protected the existence of their means of credit. Peyton objected to having to take wildcat notes from an obscure Atlanta bank as change. The hotelkeeper refused to honor Peyton's preference, proclaiming:

> Why, sir, . . . this hotel was built with that kind of stuff. . . . I will take "wild cats" for your bill, my butcher takes them of me, and the farmer from him, and so we go, making it pleasant all around. I only take care . . . to invest what I may have at the end of a given time in corner lots. . . . On this kind of worthless currency, based on Mr. Smith's [the issuer's] supposed wealth and our wants, we are creating a great city, building up all kind of industrial establishments, and covering the lake with vessels—so that suffer who may when the inevitable hour of reckoning arrives, the country will be the gainer, Jack Rossiter [the speaker] will try, when this day of reckoning comes, to have "clean hands" and a fair record. . . . A man who meddles, my dear sir, with wild-cat banks is on a slippery spot, and that spot the edge of a precipice. (Peyton 1869: 605)

In a similar vein, a former governor of Illinois, Thomas Ford, recalled that although banks owed more than they could pay and although the people owed each other and the banks more than they could pay, "yet if the whole people could be persuaded to believe this incredible falsehood that all were able to pay, this was 'confidence'" (Ford 1854: 227; cited in Hammond 1947: 235).

Not surprisingly, every so often the whole system of credit explodes or collapses. At such times, the price system suddenly careens away from its expected course. For example, with the rapid expansion of credit, the credit system becomes so bloated that prices soar. During such episodes, confidence gives way to overconfidence. At other times, confidence becomes virtually nonexistent. Credit becomes scarce and prices suddenly collapse, threatening the existence of the entire system.

As Walter Bagehot, the philosopher of the British banking system once noted, "Credit—the disposition of one man to trust another—is singularly varying. In England, after a great calamity, everybody is suspicious of everybody; as soon as that calamity is forgotten, everybody again confides in everybody" (Bagehot 1873: 64).

The Instability of Finance

Few economists today accept that the sort of credit cycles that Bagehot described are a natural component of a market economy. Instead, they blandly assume that markets automatically tend to move toward a stable equilibrium. Few economists question the dogma that markets guarantee stability, while interference with markets necessarily threatens to unleash a torrent of instability.

Despite frequent episodes of financial instability, contemporary economists typically associate such events with some sort of inappropriate behavior that somehow has violated the norms of the market. The market itself is held blameless. The problems always lie elsewhere. The central bank or the government may have abused its powers by printing too much money. Bankers might have behaved imprudently. Shady businesspeople might have acted fraudulently, but the markets did nothing wrong.

In recent decades, we have been lucky. The economy has weathered these temporary outbreaks of financial instability without setting off a major worldwide catastrophe, such as the Great Depression. Given that the world has not experienced a repetition of the Great Depression for more than six decades, economists might feel justified in not having put much thought into questions about the instability of finance. Rather than directly addressing the question of the stability of the financial system, economists spend a great deal of time and effort on a somewhat related issue—the theory of inflation.

While modern economists seem nonchalant about the risk of overall financial instability, they appear to be acutely sensitive to the threat of inflation. Economists generally lay the blame for inflation on fiscal or monetary malfeasance on the part of the state or the central bank. Unfortunately, bemoaning the evils of supposedly government-induced inflation does little to explain either the nature of the instability or the stability of prices. A cynic might suspect that self-interest is at work here. Perhaps economists give so much thought to inflation because it threatens the wealthy owners of bonds, whom economists hold in higher regard than some of the less fortunate sectors of society.

Many economists are quick to emphasize the distortions that inflation imposes on the economy. They insist that inflation makes price signals hard to interpret. They often allude to pathological cases, such as the German hyperinflation of the early 1920s, when workers were paid in wheelbarrows of virtually worthless money.

In any case, economists often become uncharacteristically emotional about the subject of inflation. Jacques Reuff, an economist closely associated with Charles DeGaulle, once claimed that price instability is one of the main causes of the weakness of civilization (Reuff 1964: 30). An even more extravagant claim came from James Buchanan and Richard E. Wagner, the former a Nobel laureate. They attributed to inflation, in part the:

> general erosion of public and private manners, increasingly liberalized attitudes toward sexual activities, a declining vitality of the Puritan work ethic, deterioration in product quality, explosion of the welfare roles, widespread corruption in both the private and governmental sector, and, finally, observed increases of the voters from the political process. . . . [W]ho can deny that inflation, itself one of the consequence of that conversion, plays some role in reinforcing several of the observed behavior patterns?
>
> Inflation destroys expectations and creates uncertainty; it increases the sense of felt injustice and causes alienation. It prompts behavioral responses that reflect a generalized shortening of time horizons. "Enjoy, enjoy"—the imperative of our time—becomes a rational response in a setting where tomorrow remains insecure and where the plans made yesterday seem to have been made in folly. (Buchanan and Wagner 1977: 64–65)

In truth, modest levels of inflation do not seem to hurt economic growth rates at all. The losses from corporate waste, monopolistic practices, and most of all, human potential, all weigh far heavier on the economy than the supposed losses from modest levels of inflation.

Although some economists have been able to build models that find some evidence of harm from low levels of inflation, many other models find none. In fact, quite a bit evidence suggests that modest levels of inflation actually help the economy by making adjustments easier. For example, when a firm is in decline, it may not have to cut wages. With modest levels of inflation, merely holding wages steady will result in an erosion of workers' buying power without creating the sort of conflict associated with a direct attack on wages (see Palley 1997; Akerlof, Dickens, and Perry 1996; and Stanners 1996).

In reality, events associated with a collapse in prices are far more disturbing than a typical inflationary regime. Although economists often attempt to pin the blame for deflation, as well as inflation, on prior missteps of the state or the central bank, their efforts are not always convincing.

They never even consider the possibility that instability might be endemic to the economic system.

The theory of inflation does not represent a threat to the discipline of economics. Unlike the distortions associated with x-inefficiency, the distortions associated with inflation are consistent with an equilibrium-based theory.

Strangely enough, I have never seen any economist even attempt a realistic explanation of why we should expect overall price stability to be the normal case in a modern economy, except for interference by the government or monetary authorities. Instead, what we find is a story of why relative prices should be stable in a world without money, credit, fixed capital, or even time. The result is less than satisfying.

In contrast, I will argue that the imposition of some sort of anchor—that is, a nonmarket force—is required for stability.

Deflation

Although the damages that deflation imposes on society exceed those caused by inflation, economists rarely address the subject of deflation. Rather than appeal to the abstraction of distorted price signals, let us trace out the real impact of a deflationary spiral.

Keep in mind that all prices do not fall during a deflation. The most glaring exception is the price of a debt. A loan contracted for $1,000 still requires payment in full. Many firms will be unable to meet their debt obligations, setting off a chain of bankruptcies that can make a depression far more severe than it might otherwise be (Bernanke 1983 and 1981; Keynes 1930, vi: 344). While falling prices might make savers wealthier, they also make borrowers poorer. Since debtors presumably are more inclined to spend than creditors are, demand should contract (Tobin 1980: 9ff).

Even more well-off firms are unlikely to invest a great deal during an economic crisis. After all, business is already down. Those firms that are most financially strapped risk becoming insolvent. They are especially inclined to postpone investments.

Finally, if the experience of recent deflation convinces firms and households that still more deflation is likely, they will have even more reason not to spend. By waiting to spend, they can take advantage of lower expected costs in the future. This lack of investment and consumption creates a substantial drag on the economy. Consumers will also witness an evaporation of the value of assets they own. For example, the value of their homes will shrink without any offsetting decline in their mortgage payments (Mishkin 1977 and 1978; see also Gramm 1972). This effect will make the contraction of demand more intense.

As a result, we can conclude that, to the extent that firms or individuals attempt to get out from under debt by spending less or by selling more, they merely reinforce the deadly deflationary spiral. In the words of Irving Fisher: "*The very effort of individuals to lessen their burden of debts increases it, because of the mass effect of the stampede to liquidate in swelling each dollar owed.* Then we have the great paradox which, I submit, is the chief secret of most, if not all, great depressions. *The more debtors pay, the more they owe*" (Fisher 1933: 344).

What, then, could cause an economy to fall into a deflationary spiral?

Equilibrium and Instability

As we have already noted, most economic models assume away the likelihood of a serious instability. Instead, they presume that the economy always has a strong tendency to move toward an equilibrium state. If something pushes the economy away from an equilibrium, pressures will automatically build up within the economy to counteract them. For example, if a price begins to rise above its equilibrium level, producers will respond briskly to the increased profit opportunity that the higher price presents and supply more of the good. The increase in the supply will automatically tend to drive the price back down.

This abstract example works, in part, because everyone's behavior is self-evident. In the context of a simple economic model, the price signal reveals everything anybody needs to know. In reality, price information is more complex. In the language of economics, prices are asymmetric. Even if one party knows the true conditions, the other can only infer what the situation is. In a world of asymmetric information, markets can amplify mistakes rather than correct them.

Consider an example from the world of finance. Suppose for some unknown reason somebody suddenly withholds credit from a business. The managers suddenly scour around for an alternative source of credit. Lenders ask them why they are in need at this particular time; why did their credit suddenly dry up? The lenders do not and cannot not have full information about the business, so they have to rely on external information. The fact that the previous lender withdrew credit might very well be a signal that something is amiss at the firm.

As a result, lenders withhold credit and our firm goes bankrupt, putting its suppliers under pressure. Further suppose that some of them go under. Banks, seeing that business failures are on the rise, become more stingy with their loans, putting still more businesses under still more pressure. Within a short period of time, this contagion can cascade out of control, leaving the economy in a state of depression.

The typical economic model rules out the possibility that simple mistakes can take on a momentum of their own. Instead, they presume that mistakes will cancel themselves out or that self-regulating market forces will correct the mistakes. Unfortunately, these models rest on assumptions that are both severe and unrealistic.

Now let us return to the question about why prices should tend to be stable. If money still consisted of livestock or another commodity, then the standard theory of equilibrium would indeed imply that prices would be stable. Unfortunately, such hypothetical prices, based on commodity money, would be of little use in understanding a modern economy. Instead, they would merely demonstrate the theory of price setting in a hypothetical barter economy.

In fact, for the most part, the typical mainstream theory of price is actually little more than an analysis of how prices will be set in a barter economy. In a modern monetary economy with extensive credit, such a theory of equilibrium prices might offer some comfort for those whose faith in the market economy is tied up with a belief in a tendency for price stability; however, this theory will do little to enlighten us about the real economy.

Within this sort of theory, credit is virtually irrelevant; money merely acts as a measuring rod, the dimensions of which might expand and fall with the state of the credit system. For example, given the existing technologies (including weather conditions) and demand structure, the price of an orange relative to the price of an apple should be a fixed ratio. Let us assume that both are worth a dime.

Imagine that a financial panic suddenly begins. These panics do happen in the real world, even though we cannot agree on the cause. Fearful of the future, people will want to hold more money. As a result, prices collapse. Even so, the price ratio of apples and oranges may be unaffected. A piece of either kind of fruit, which had previously cost a dime, may still cost a nickel or a penny.

If financial panics left the entire structure of prices unaffected, they would be of little concern. Indeed, if a financial panic remained only that—a panic concerning financial matters—the structure of prices would have only a passing interest. Unfortunately, in the real world, financial panics can easily spin out of control into a full-blown crisis.

Now we shall turn to a discussion of how economists go beyond the theory of static equilibrium, while virtually ruling out the possibility of any fundamental instability.

CHAPTER 3

Cycles: Stability Within Instability

Models of Cycles

Earlier, I made the assertion that the modern discipline of economics is ill suited to the study of the dynamic nature of the economy. This assertion should not be too surprising. After all, economic dynamism, let alone economic instability, seems to defy the sort simple explanations that static economic models offer.

People want to understand the calamities that they encounter. The search for an explanation of calamities began in antiquity. Ancient peoples, seeing in the heavens a stability and a regularity that probably seemed absent from their precarious earthly lives, tried to make sense of their world. They imagined that their fates depended on the moods of gods up above. They looked to the planets for signals about the intentions of the gods.

As the market played a larger role in people's lives, people began to try to comprehend economic crises. Nonetheless, in the centuries that followed the end of antiquity, the world witnessed little progress in understanding economic instability. Prior to the economic collapse of 1847, people did not seem to associate crises with the workings of the market. The irregular appearance of some outside cause, such as wars, technical change, or speculative manias, always seemed to be responsible for each economic crisis (Kuznets 1930a: 382). Any general theory of instability seemed to be out of the question.

Following the crisis of 1847, this perspective changed. For many observers, some force internal to the market economy seemed to cause a never-ending cycle of booms and busts. As the impact of these recurrent crises seemed to get more and more violent, they cried out for an explanation.

Satisfactory explanations proved elusive, in part because of economists' tendency to look at separate parts of the economy. For example, economists generally divide the financial or monetary parts from the rest of the economy, which they call the "real economy." Of course, both monetary and real forces can trigger crises, although pinpointing the exact cause is no easy matter.

I already mentioned that economists still debate the cause of these earlier episodes. For example, either overproduction or lack of demand can cause widespread bankruptcies in the financial sector. In the event of such a crisis, some economists will blame the crisis on the real forces and others on monetary forces, very much like the proverbial blind men attempting to identify an elephant. In truth, we need to look at the economy as a whole.

Over the years, economists offered up a variety of plausible theories of economic crises. Some contended that catastrophes reappear with some degree of regularity because of mysterious, long, cyclical waves that sweep across the economy every half century for no particular reason. Others blame the financial system that channels funds into too many inappropriate ventures, which cannot repay their debts. Others point to a maldistribution of income that does not permit workers to purchase enough of their production. Still others proposed that the system had an inherent tendency to result in economic crises.

For the most part, economists put themselves in an ideological bind. They generally feel a need to justify the market economy at the same time that they try to explain why the economy would lead to a crisis. How, then, could economists meet the challenge of providing an account of the admirable nature of the economy and still do so in a scientific manner that would take the fact of recurrent crises into account?

At the same time, most economists displayed a desire to solidify their position within influential sectors of society. As a result, they were not overly eager to lay blame in the direction of the rich and the powerful. By recasting their theories so that these crises appeared to be part of a less-menacing natural phenomenon, markets would seem more palatable. One early twentieth-century economist, Joseph Schumpeter, even welcomed the instability as an indication of the introduction of new technology that revolutionizes the economy. However, as we shall see later, his work presented far deeper challenges to economic theory in other respects.

Some economists noted that these crises seemed to recur with some regularity. As a result, "During the nineteenth century crisis theory evolved into trade-cycle theory" (Hagemann and Landesmann 1997: 116). Their strategy was to reassure citizens that the apparent instability was actually a regular pattern. Just as the pattern of seasonal change does not indicate a change in the overall climate, the seeming regularity of a business cycle has more in common with stability than instability.

If economists could unravel the mystery of the cycle and explain the business cycle as a natural phenomenon, then they could encompass the seemingly erratic behavior of the economy within the context of a scientific model. After all, science is an attempt to discover the natural laws of the world around us. Of course, nobody ever thought that the business cycle displayed the same degree of regularity of a planetary cycle or even the regularity of the seasons, but the regularity seemed sufficiently strong to suggest the existence of some underlying law of economic cycles, akin to the planetary laws of motion—a law that might explain the ebb and flow of economic activity.

To the extent that economists could uncover the underlying law of the business cycle, they could accomplish two not entirely different goals. To begin with, their scientific credentials would be strengthened. In addition, they could reassure those who were skeptical about the market. Within the context of the business cycle, the ups and downs of the economy only appear to indicate instability, much like a roller coaster gives the illusion of heading for a crash while offering relative safety for its occupants.

The Search for the Cycle

Economists have proposed numerous alternative explanations for the business cycle, ranging from the changes in the physical environment to the need for periodic replacement of capital goods, monetary phenomena, and speculative activity, as well as swings in psychological moods. I have purposely chosen the order of these suspected causes of the business cycle to represent a movement from purely physical influences to more subjective factors. Notice that economic analysis is most appropriate to those factors that fall in the middle of this list, since economics is not particularly well suited to explain either physical laws or psychological behavior.

As early as 1829, George MacKenzie proposed that solar activity drove a 54-year cycle in the price of wheat. Then, in 1847, Dr. Hyde Clarke published a paper, "Physical Economy," in the *British Railway Journal* that supported MacKenzie's "circle" of wheat prices. Clarke speculated that the "cyclar period of famine" was related to fluctuations in the earth's electromagnetic field (Klein 1997: 113; see also Mager 1987: 21).

Ten years later, in 1857, William Langton, founder of the Manchester Statistical Society, reported that he found statistical evidence that cycles appear more or less regularly at ten-year intervals (Peart 1991: 246). Not long thereafter, William Stanley Jevons, who was teaching in Manchester, attempted to reduce economic fluctuations to cycles of solar activity (Jevons 1879). Jevons reasoned that solar conditions affected the weather, which in turn affected agricultural yields, which were then the decisive factor in determining the level of economic activity.

Jevons became perhaps the most important figure in the reformulation of economics as a mathematically based discipline. He hoped that his analysis of the business cycle would encourage economists to cease looking for economic causes of instability and instead concentrate on what he considered to be the science of economics; namely, how market incentives induced firms and households to behave in a way that would maximize utility (see Mirowski 1984: 47). According to Jevons:

> We must lay to the charge of trades-unions, or free trade, or any other pretext, a fluctuation of commerce which affects countries alike which have trades-unions and no trades-unions, free trade and protection: as to intemperance and various other moral causes, no doubt they may have a powerful influence on our prosperity, but they afford no special explanation of a temporary wave of calamity. (Jevons 1879: 91; cited in Mirowski 1984: 47; see also Jevons 1882)

In effect, then, Jevons' theory of the cycle was an attempt to put such subjects to rest. Because noneconomic forces caused the disruptive cycle, economists were free to forsake study of the cycle to concentrate their attention on the beneficial workings of supply and demand.

Even Jevons must have seen that the basis for his theory was shrinking at the time he was writing. The agricultural share of overall economic activity was in sharp decline. For example, the 1880 census of the United States was the last one in which agriculture employed more than half of U.S. workers. As a result, sunspots were directly affecting a shrinking portion of the overall economy. In fact, Jevons himself earlier expressed fears that shortages of industrial raw materials, especially coal, could pose the ultimate economic threat (Jevons 1865).

In the early years of the twentieth century, Henry Moore developed a more sophisticated analysis of weather patterns correlating agricultural yields with the transit of Venus. Although Moore was very learned in the literature of physics and economics, elite economists responded to his work with disgust. Although Moore was the founder of modern statistical economics, his astronomical approach was anathema to his colleagues, who wanted, above all, for economics to achieve the status of a science. Astronomical phenomena seemed a bit too much like astrology for their tastes (see Mirowski 1988).

In the fall of 1918, Moore was stripped of his research position at Columbia University. He was assigned to the chair of economics and sociology at Barnard and was required to abandon teaching mathematical and statistical economics for courses in sociology and the history of feminism (Mirowski 1988). Posterity was no kinder to Moore, whose contributions to economics are almost completely forgotten.

Modern economists treat Jevons' work with far more respect. They generally acknowledge him as one of the main founders of the modern mainstream economics. Even so, most economists today consign Jevons' theory of the sunspot cycle to a footnote in the history of economics, the point of which is usually to show how naïve even our most distinguished forbears were.

Moore's colleague, Wesley Claire Mitchell, later took up Moore's work on the business cycle but without the astronomical explanation (Mitchell 1913). While working as research director for the National Bureau of Economic Research, an institution that he helped to organize, Mitchell gathered an enormous amount of data to develop his theory of the business cycle. Mitchell's cycles did not display an absolute regularity. In fact, he regarded each cycle as unique, even though every one followed the same pattern of nine stages (Sherman 1991: 11).

Although economists never wrote Mitchell off as a crank or a crackpot, many considered his work a failure. One of the most famous attacks came from a Dutch physicist-turned economist, Tjalling Koopmans, who described Mitchell's work as "Measurement without Theory" (Koopmans 1947). If economics is to be scientific, then merely describing a business cycle was of no value whatsoever. Mitchell supposedly had the obligation to give an economic reason for the pattern of business cycles.

In effect, the discipline of economics was setting an impossible task for itself. It aspired to be scientific. To be scientific, economists insisted that a theory had to be based on a formal economic model. In addition, the model could not challenge the deeply held beliefs that markets work well. The only way such a model could work would be for it to prove that business cycles do not occur.

Monetary Models of the Cycle

People who were less attached to the idealizing of market societies approached cycles in a somewhat different fashion. The year after Langton's address, Karl Marx wrote a letter about the nature of the cycle to his friend, Frederick Engels, who, like Jevons, lived and worked in Manchester. Marx suggested that the economy followed a ten-year business cycle because the average piece of equipment lasted ten years. Marx noted that this approach had the added advantage of locating the engine of the cycle within large-scale industry (Marx to Engels, 5 March 1858; in Marx and Engels 1983: 40: 282–84).

Four years later, just after asking Engels to visit in order to help him with details on his book, *Contribution to the Critique of Political Economy,* Marx again brought up the question of the durability of fixed capital (Marx to Engels, 20 August 1862; in Marx and Engels 1973, 30: 279–81; see also Marx to Engels, 7 May 1868; in Marx and Engels 1973: 32: 82; and Engels to Marx, 10 May 1868; in Marx and Engels 1973: 32: 83–85).

Engels, whose family firm was close to bankruptcy because of the scarcity of cotton due to the Civil War in the United States, expressed impatience with Marx's notion that plant and equipment would normally wear out in ten years. He even suggested that Marx had "gone off the rails." Depreciation time is not, of course, the same for all machines (Engels to Marx, 9 September, 1862; in Marx and Engels 1985: 414).

Atypically, Marx never absorbed Engels' lessons on the irregular turnover of plant and equipment. Instead, he frequently referred to the decennial cycles brought on by the pattern of renewing fixed capital (see, for example, Marx 1967, 2: 185–86; and 1963–1971, Pt. 1: 699).

To his credit, Marx did what Wesley Mitchell did not do. He gave an economic reason for the cycle. Even though, as Engels well knew, Marx was wrong, the seemingly scientific approach he applied made this aspect of his theory attractive to others, including many who were unsympathetic to virtually everything else that Marx stood for.

A Ukrainian economist, Mikhail Ivanovich Tugan-Baranovski, adopted Marx's theory of crises, then passed it on to influential mainstream economists, such as Gustav Cassel of Sweden, Arthur Spiethoff of Germany, and Dennis H. Robertson of England (Hayek 1941: 426). By such routes, Marx's cycle theory surreptitiously entered mainstream economics.

Another theory of business cycles concerned money and banking. This version of the business cycle was not necessarily threatening to economists, because it did not call markets into question. Presumably, within the context of the monetary cycle, society could bring the deficiencies of the monetary system under control with the proper legislation. As a result, markets supposedly could provide perpetual prosperity without the interruption of crises.

The famed Swedish economist and social reformer, Knut Wicksell, provided the nuts and bolts of the modern version of this theory (Schumpeter 1954: 1118–20). Because both money and the credits of the banking system (say, checks) affect demand in the same way, the monetary and banking authorities provide the bulk of the buying power in the economy. According to Wicksell, an economy can sustain a limited rate of growth for an extended period. He named the level of interest that would encourage this growth rate the "natural rate of interest." If the rate that the banking system charges falls below this level, imbalances will build up, eventually causing the economy to decline. So long as the interest rate coincides with the natural rate, the economy could be trouble free.

With the money and banking approach to the business cycle, human shortcomings rather than natural causes begin to explain the cycle, but these imperfections are limited to bankers or those who regulate monetary policy.

Speculation and Crises

Those who attributed the cycle to speculation allowed for a broader role for human deficiency. Of course, economists have long realized that speculation is major element in economic activity. According to Adam Smith, "The establishment of any new manufacture, of any new branch of commerce . . . is always a speculation, from which the projector promises himself extraordinary profits. These profits are sometimes very great, and sometimes, more frequently, perhaps, they are quite otherwise; but in general they bear no regular proportion to those of other old trades in the neighborhood" (Smith 1776, I.x.b.43: 131–2).

Most of us have seen some location in a town where one shop after another fails. Each new venture opens up with some fanfare, seemingly exuding confidence that it will succeed where its numerous predecessors have faltered. Why, then, are so many investors willing to speculate when the failure rate is so high? Here again, we can turn to Adam Smith for some insight into this riddle. He observed:

> The over-weening conceit which the greater part of men have of their own abilities, is an ancient evil remarked by the philosophers and moralists of all

> ages. Their absurd presumption in their own good fortune, has been less taken notice of it. It is, however, if possible, still more universal. . . . The chance of gain is by every man more or less over-valued, and the chance of loss is by most men under-valued. (Smith 1776, I.x.b.26: 124–5)

So Smith attributed the frequency of unsuccessful investments to a common character defect, one that causes most people to overestimate their luck. He was not alone in his recognition of the tendency to overestimate good fortune. His contemporary, Samuel Johnson, also displayed an acute awareness of this all-too-human failing. Boswell, Johnson's famous biographer, reçounts a wonderful example of Johnson's insight. Thrale, the great brewer, had appointed Johnson one of his executors. In that capacity it became his duty to sell the business after Thrale's demise. When the sale was about to go on, Boswell reported, "Johnson appeared bustling about, with an inkhorn and pen in his button-hole, like an exciseman, and on being asked what he really considered to be the value of the property which was to be disposed of, answered—'We are not here to sell a parcel of vats and boilers, but the *Potentiality* of growing rich beyond the dreams of avarice'" (Boswell 1964, vol. 6: 85–86)

Smith himself realized that the "dreams of avarice" are not constant. He observed, "When the profits of trade happen to be greater than ordinary, overtrading becomes a general error both among great and small dealers" (Smith 1776, IV.i.16: 437–8).

John Stuart Mill, perhaps the most prominent economist of the middle of the nineteenth century, continued with the same theme, noting, "Some accident which excites expectations of rising prices, such as the opening of a new foreign market, or simultaneous indications of a short supply of several great articles of commerce . . . sets speculations at work in several leading departments at once" (Mill 1848, 3: 542).

Although speculation seems like an obvious candidate for introducing at least some instability into the economy, economists prefer to downplay its importance. Their models generally presume that people are rational. The assumption of rationality, of course, allows economic models to behave with more regularity. Once we allow irrationality to enter into the equation, simple models lose whatever justification they may have.

Consequently, speculation is an inconvenient subject for economists. After all, how could you build a science of economics on a foundation of irrational and erratic behavior? With such considerations in mind, economists had good reason to wish to build a cycle theory that would be consistent with rational behavior.

Simon Kuznets and the Role of Lags in the Business Cycle

In 1930, before the Great Depression had reached its peak of devastation, Simon Kuznets offered a new analysis of the erratic movements of the economy. His explanation depended on the complications caused by the time required to respond to changes in supply and demand (Kuznets 1930a).

Anyone who has had trouble adjusting the temperature of water while taking a shower can understand what Kuznets meant. When we adjust the water temperature, the full impact of our actions occurs with a delay. Now think about how this slow feedback can cause us to overshoot. Imagine that we have just put on more hot water. Even though the water hitting our body may still be too cool for our comfort, the water in the pipes may already be too hot. Having no way of realizing the temperature of the water still in the pipes, we may continue to make the water hotter. To our regret, we learn of our error when the uncomfortably hot water hits our body. In effect, then, even in this simple example, the achievement of an equilibrium is no easy matter.

Kuznets concluded his article, "Equilibrium Economics and Business Cycle Theory," by laying down a challenge for his fellow economists, "If we are to develop any effective general theory of economic change and any complete theory of economic behavior, the practice of treating change as a deviation from an imaginary picture of a rigid equilibrium system must be abandoned" (1930a: 415).

In other words, economists stubbornly insist on using models that presume the economy is in an equilibrium or about to reach an equilibrium. In these imaginary equilibria situations, all resources are fully employed, even though economies do no behave that way in reality. Given the unreality of the models of equilibrium, Kuznets' complaint seems more than reasonable. After all, at the time his article appeared, the world still had another decade of depression ahead of it.

At the time of the article under discussion, Kuznets was working for Wesley Mitchell's National Bureau of Economic Research, which also emphasized empirical rather than theoretical economics. Some years later, Kuznets praised Mitchell for his "distrust of formalism, . . . recognition of complexity of historical reality, . . . (and) awareness of limitations of the human mind unchecked by objectively recorded data" (Kuznets 1947: 144).

Kuznets, in one of the rare acknowledgments of the importance of Henry Moore, said that economists could still study equilibria, but only if they took the cycle into account (Kuznets 1930a: 397). Kuznets' claim might sound confused. Is he saying that we should or we should not study equilibrium conditions? In fact, Kuznets' point was rather commonsensical. Think of how we talk about the weather in everyday life. We know that temperature varies with the seasons. In the northern hemisphere, a warm December is likely to be colder than a cool July. We can compare one December day with another December day from a previous year. In this way, we can eliminate the effect of the seasons, to study the normal weather pattern.

The National Bureau of Economic Research wanted to discover the normal pattern of a business cycle—what they referred to as a "reference cycle." Kuznets had to know that many economists found fault with a similar approach. Although we can talk about a cold summer or a warm winter, creating an exact measure of a normal year is no easy matter. What recourse, then, did economists have if they were to choose to follow his lead?

Since, as Kuznets argued, the existence of lags made equilibrium virtually impossible, economic fluctuations are inevitable, economists should accept that economic fluctuations are a normal part of the economy, just as the seasons are part of our weather pattern. In the early years of the Great Depression, that path might not have been particularly inviting.

So, despite his clear call to abandon equilibrium theory, Kuznets never made much of a mark on pure economic theory. Instead, economists justly recognized him as a prodigious gatherer and organizer of data. Decades later, he won a Nobel Prize for this empirical work.

The Mathematics of the Illusory Cycle

Suppose that the undulations of the economy were nothing but a statistical fluke? This suggestion leads us back to Wicksell, whom we met in discussing the monetary cycle. Wicksell used a simple analogy to illustrate a rather complex mathematical point. In a Swedish publication in 1918, he noted that "If one hits a rocking-horse with a hammer, then the movements of the rocking horse become very different from that of the hammer" (Boianovsky 1995: 382). In other words, random events, rather than canceling each other out, may act cumulatively to create economic cycles.

About a decade and a half later, in 1927, just before the Great Depression, Eugen Slutsky gave a formal mathematical proof that random processes could lead to a business cycle. A decade later, an English translation of this article appeared in *Econometrica,* the most prestigious technical economics journal in the United States (Slutsky 1937). This theory eventually became popular among economists despite the unfortunate timing of its appearance, because it seemed to achieve Jevons' goal of framing cycles as a normal phenomenon, rather than as a defect in the organization of our economy.

One would still need to explain why the structure of the economy is such that these cycles appear. Why would the errors not cancel each other out instead of creating cycles? Returning to Wicksell's metaphor, hammering on a large block of wood will not necessarily produce the same cycles as would occur after the block is carved into a rocking horse. Depending on the size and shape of the block, it can slide or topple in response to a blow. Does a market economy have any particular structural feature that makes it behave more like a rocking horse rather than a block of wood?

These business cycle questions were more than mental fodder for isolated academics. The 1917 Soviet Revolution was fresh in people's memories. The Great Depression called the capitalist organization of society into question, because a socialist economy would seem to be immune from the ravages of a depression.

If Slutsky were correct, that the cycle was merely the result of the adding of small random causes together with time delays, then people might just as well weather the Depression rather than risk changing the entire economic system. On the other hand, if the Depression represented a collapse of the entire system, as many people thought to be the case at the time, then something was certainly wrong with the system as a whole and society would have to face serious political questions.

A Concluding Note on Crises

Well before Adam Smith had begun to inoculate future economists against a concern with crises, the study of the economy as such, as distinguished from the whole range of social conditions, began to emerge. At the time, independent economic forces had become more prominent relative to custom and tradition. In addition, crises seemed to have become more common. Just as we think about a particular organ of our body more seriously after it malfunctions, we pay more attention to the economy when it falls into a crisis.

Economists have always been torn between the twin objectives of knowledge and comfort. Their work on crises was no different in this regard. To the extent that they were engaged in an effort to understand the economy scientifically, they had to come to grips with the problem of crises; to the extent that they wanted to propagandize in favor of markets, economists wanted to calm the disquiet that the market economy provoked. For the most part, the latter motivation won out.

So, for the most part, these early economists, like their more modern counterparts, devoted their energies to showing why crises would not happen or even trying to prove that crises were impossible. Only recently, medical scientists had discovered how blood circulated through the body. The analogy of the circulatory system was especially attractive since it suggested that the economy could remain in balance, free from crises.

Some of the most prominent early economists also happened to be doctors, including Sir William Petty (1623–1687), John Locke (1632–1704), and Francois Quesnay (1694–1774). These early economists often used the metaphor of circulation to describe how goods and money move through the economy. To this day, we still speak of money circulating through the economy.

Quesnay had actually published works concerning the human circulatory system prior to his economic writings. Later, he built on this work by constructing an interesting model of the circulation of goods to show how a stagnant economy could grow while remaining in balance.

Whereas Quesnay's work points toward an economics of stability, Locke opened the door for crises in pointing out how the durability of money changed the very nature of economic activity. Locke's point is easy to understand. We can appreciate the importance of Locke's approach by considering how a nondurable money would affect the economy.

Suppose that we used a perishable good, such as fish, as money. In the absence of refrigeration, nobody would want to hoard money. As soon as people received money, they would want to spend it. Nobody would have any incentive to become rich by accumulating money. People would still want more land or bigger houses, but money as such would have no value whatsoever, except for its ability to be exchanged for goods right away.

In this environment, purely economic crises would not occur. Producers as a whole could not be stuck with too many goods. An individual might be set back if she made too many shoes or even the wrong kind of shoes, but producers in general could not manufacture too many goods because people would always want to spend their money immediately.

The difference between fish money and money as we know it is that fish money eliminates much of the influence of time. Each day, all the money will be spent because tomorrow it will have no use. In effect, then, a fish money economy becomes similar to a barter economy. The fish are useful for keeping score and then for eating, but not for long. No one need be unemployed because of a lack of money in the economy. If too few fish are caught, the fish price of goods will be lower. In effect, each fish will be worth more.

In the case of the shoemaker, her shoes need not remain unsold. She might get fewer fish for her shoes than she expected, but she can probably sell them. Even if nobody wants them at any price, she can start over tomorrow, making shoes or doing something else. Nobody need be unemployed.

We can still allow a temporal element into our economy. The shoemaker could put some of her shoes into an inventory. She could devote some of her time to pursuing a different profession until she works off her shoe inventory. Even so, we would not expect to see an economic crisis.

In contrast, people can hoard durable money. This hoarding, in turn, can lead to crises. Now, Locke was not studying crises as such. He was merely trying to understand how the use of money promoted investment.

Even so, Locke's work pointed to one of the most troubling features of these economic crises which is the paradoxical situation in which business has too many goods on hand, while people are too poor to buy these same goods. During these crises, money, not goods, seems to be in short supply.

Economists devoted a considerable amount of energy in the early nineteenth century to close the door that Locke had opened. In this regard, economists satisfied themselves by pointing out that because every purchase was a sale, and every sale a purchase, they could rule out the possibility of economic imbalances. Economists refer to this conclusion as "Say's Law," after Jean-Baptiste Say (1767–1832). Say's contemporary, David Ricardo, penned the most famous formulation of Say's Law, explaining, "No man produces, but with a view to consume or sell, and he never sells but with an intention to purchase some other commodity. . . . By producing, then, he necessarily becomes either the consumer of his own goods, or the purchaser and consumer of the goods of some other person" (Ricardo 1817: 290).

In truth, Say was not as superficial as the later economists who swore allegiance to the principle of Say's Law (see Uchitelle 1998). Even so, a century after his work, Say's Law was still accepted by most economists without reservation.

The Great Depression cast doubt on Say's Law and renewed interest in both cycles and crises. Since then, economists have been hard at work trying to rehabilitate Say's Law and putting all fears of economic crises to rest once again.

Not all economists followed this path. We shall now turn to them.

CHAPTER 4

Instability: Keynes, Schumpeter, Polanyi, and the Passenger Pigeon

Keynes

Keynes' General Theory and Instability

As I mentioned earlier, the regularity that a cyclical pattern represents suggests a form of stability. The instability that I want to discuss goes beyond cyclical behavior.

If the business-cycle theory cannot help us to understand economic instability, where do we look to find assistance in getting a handle on this subject? Among modern economists, the first name that would probably come up in a discussion of instability would be John Maynard Keynes. When most economists think of Keynes, his most famous book, *The General Theory of Employment, Interest and Money* (1936), comes to mind.

Keynes' great merit was to draw our attention to the absence of any economic forces that would drive the economy toward a full-employment equilibrium. Where Jevons blamed economic instability on solar activity in an attempt to banish human psychology from economic analysis, Keynes, in his book, insisted on returning to the psychological foundations of economic behavior. Although psychological changes might have triggered the Depression, the psychological state showed no sign of improving at the time. As Keynes noted, "The state of long term expectation is often steady, and, even when it is not, the other factors exert their compensating effects" (Keynes 1936: 162).

In this sense, we could say that Keynes' masterwork is not particularly useful in our quest to understand instability. Writing in the midst of the Great Depression, the prospect of stability rather than instability troubled

Keynes. After all, the world was mired in a depression, which seemed to be distressingly stable. So, we could classify Keynes as a theoretician of economic stability, albeit of an unwelcome sort of stability.

Keynes did address instability in the sense that he observed that an economy could fall into a depression at any moment, but he did not go very far in analyzing this instability. Beyond pointing to what he called "animal spirits," Keynes did not offer much insight into why depressions would recur. Keynes merely proclaimed that these animal spirits could run high for an extended period and then become stagnant for years on end. Although Keynes differed from Jevons in emphasizing psychology, in the end, like Jevons, he attributed depressions to noneconomic forces that were beyond his ken.

Underlying Keynes' analysis of animal spirits was a "pop psychology" interpretation of class. For Keynes, money-grubbing businessmen were classic subjects of the Freudian analysis of anal compulsiveness. Keynes preferred to have major economic decisions made by public-spirited members of the elite. Keynes gives the impression that he believed that such individuals, by virtue of their culture, superb education, and overall effortless superiority, supposedly would be more or less immune from the undue influence of animal spirits.

I do not mean to belittle the economic influence of psychology in the market. My dissatisfaction with Keynes stems from his insistence that the forces that cause instability necessarily lie outside of the market. I accept that some nonmarket forces—Keynes' animal spirits or natural disruptions, such as earthquakes, floods, or even Jevons' sunspots—all can cause instability. Over and above such disruptions, I insist that forces internal to the markets also cause economic instability, notwithstanding the views of Jevons, Keynes, and the vast majority of modern economists.

Keynes' Earlier Musings on Instability

Ironically, Keynes paid more attention to the subject of instability earlier, in the period following the end of World War I, than he did during the Great Depression. At the time, he warned: "Modern individualistic society, organised on lines of capitalistic industry, cannot support a violently fluctuating standard of value, whether the movement is upwards or downwards. Its arrangements presume and absolutely require a reasonably stable standard. Unless we can give it such a standard, this society will be stricken with a mortal disease and will not survive" (Keynes 1923b: 117).

Keynes suggested that the danger was not merely economic: "Only by wisely regulating the creation of currency and credit along new lines, can we protect society against the attacks of Socialist and Communist innovators" (Keynes 1923b: 117).

About the same time, in his *A Tract on Monetary Reform,* Keynes declared the monetary instability of the time to be a world-historical event: "The fluctuations in the value of money since 1914 have been on a scale so vast as to constitute . . . one of the most significant events in the economic history of the modern world" (Keynes 1923a: 1).

Keynes' concerns with the revolutionary consequences of unstable money date back a few years earlier. In the work through which Keynes first became a well-recognized national figure, *The Economic Consequences of the Peace,* he wrote:

> Lenin is said to have declared that the best way to destroy the capitalist system was to debauch the currency. By a continuing process of inflation, governments can confiscate, secretly and unobserved, an important part of the wealth of their citizens. By this method they not only confiscate, but they confiscate arbitrarily; and, while the process impoverishes many, it actually enriches some. The sight of this arbitrary rearrangement of riches strikes not only at security, but at confidence in the equity of the existing distribution of wealth. Those to whom the system brings windfalls beyond their deserts and even beyond their expectations and desires, become "profiteers," who are the object of hatred of the bourgeoisie, whom the inflationism has impoverished, not less than of the proletariat. As the inflation proceeds and the real value of the currency fluctuates wildly from month to month, all permanent relations between debtors and creditors, which form the ultimate foundation of capitalism, become so utterly disordered as to be almost meaningless, and the process of wealth-getting degenerates into a gamble and a lottery. (Keynes 1919: 149)

This long citation is important in several respects. Although Lenin does not seem to have actually made any such pronouncement (Fetter 1977), reference to Lenin and the two-year-old Bolshevik revolution suggests the reason for the importance that Keynes put on price stability. In other words, while during the Depression, stability implied a continuation of the crisis, at this earlier stage of his life, stability seemed necessary to protect the prosperity of the way of life to which Keynes was accustomed.

In addition, we can appreciate Keynes' realism compared with the almost hysterical discussion of the same subject by Buchanan and Wagner, cited earlier. More important, Keynes' words allude to a twofold fragility of the economic system. To begin with, Keynes' initial reference to Lenin highlights the subsequent allusions to the antagonisms between classes that follow. In addition, the mention of the disordering of the "permanent relations between debtors and creditors" reflects a disruption that prevents markets from functioning well. Later, Keynes explained how these two aspects of fragility are tied together: "To convert the businessman into the profiteer is to strike a blow at capitalism, because it destroys the psychological equilibrium which permits the perpetuance of unequal rewards. The economic doctrine of normal profits, vaguely apprehended by everyone, is a necessary condition for the justification of capitalism" (Keynes 1923a: 24).

The second aspect of social fragility became a common thread through much of Keynes' writings, although the first class-related element was probably never far from his mind.

In the period immediately after the publication of *The Economic Consequences,* the threat to the British economy seemed to come from other directions. England became caught up in a worldwide slump. Between 1920 and 1922, manufacturing fell about 3 percent (Moggridge 1969: 17). British industry became increasingly uncompetitive. In fact, "in nearly every major industrial category, whether expanding, declining or stable from the point of view of world trade, Britain's share in each case declined, especially between 1913 and 1929" (Aldcroft 1983: 74–5).

Ordinary people longed to return to what seemed like prewar prosperity, but British policy makers had a different vision of prosperity. Mindful of the flagging economic power of their once-great empire, they hoped to regain Britain's prewar preeminence, especially in finance. According to the financial experts in the British Treasury at the time, key to rebuilding the economy was financial stability. Specifically, the Treasury recommended returning the gold value of the British pound to its prewar level.

Keynes lead the opposition to this policy. By making British money more valuable relative to gold, British prices would have to fall considerably (see Barkai 1993). Keynes anticipated that the impending deflation would be even more dangerous than the inflation against which he warned in *The Economic Consequences:* "Thus inflation is unjust and deflation inexpedient. Of the two perhaps deflation is, if we rule out exaggerated inflations such as that of Germany, the worse; because it is worse, in an impoverished world, to provoke unemployment than to disappoint the *rentier*" (Keynes 1923a: 36).

At the time, Keynes saw grounds for hope. Prior to World War I, one could say: "The value of gold has not depended on the policy or the decisions of a single body of men; and a sufficient proportion of the supply has been able to find its way, without any flooding of the market, into the arts or into the hoards of Asia for its marginal value to be governed by a steady psychological estimation of the metal in relation to other things" (Keynes 1923a: 133).

He continued: "But the war has effected a great change. Gold itself has become a 'managed' currency. The West, as well as the East, has learnt to hoard gold" (Keynes 1923a: 134).

Presumably, Keynes thought that the world could hope to achieve monetary stability if the socially minded elites could adopt a wise international monetary policy instead of following the selfish objectives of the captains of British finance. In reality, Keynes, like anybody else, would have great difficulty in distinguishing one group from the other.

The General Strike

Reality soon shattered Keynes' hopes for monetary stability. Despite Keynes' protestations, the Chancellor of the Exchequer, Winston Churchill, announced on 28 April 1925 that Britain was returning to the pound at its prewar gold value (Skidelsky 1992: 200). Churchill himself had expressed deep fears about the wisdom of his policy, recognizing that it would create great hardship (Gilbert 1977: 97–8). In the middle of July, Keynes responded with a scathing set of articles entitled "The Economic Consequences of Mr. Churchill" (Keynes 1925). He warned: "Mr. Churchill's policy of improving the exchange by 10 percent was, sooner or later, a policy of reducing everyone's wages. . . . Deflation does not reduce wages automatically. It reduces them by causing unemployment. The proper object of dear money is to check in incipient boom. Woe to those whose faith leads them to use it to aggravate a depression" (Keynes 1925: 208 and 220).

Indeed, on 30 June, coal owners had already demanded a new agreement with the Miners' Federation that included a 10 percent wage reduction. To reduce the social tensions, Prime Minister Baldwin agreed to a subsidy that would allow the coal industry to forgo the pay cut. The subsidy was set to expire on 30 April 1926 (Skidelsky 1992: 242).

Keynes protested: "On grounds of social justice no case can be made out for reducing the wages of the miners. They are the victims of the economic juggernaut. . . . They (and others to follow) are the 'moderate sacrifice' still necessary to ensure the stability of the gold standard" (Keynes 1925: 223).

The coal industry was never far from the policy makers' minds at the time. According to one study of the industrial turmoil that followed:

> The history of the coal industry in the years from 1880 to 1926 epitomized Britain's fall from world-wide industrial supremacy. Prior to the first world war coal mining had maintained an incomparable record of growth and prosperity. Its product was both the basis of Victorian industrial enterprise and by the twentieth century the second most valuable of Britain's exports. It employed by 1914 almost one in ten of the male labour force, and afforded them more job security and higher average wages than were enjoyed in any other important occupation. It was also the subject of close political and legislative attention. By 1925, however, mining had become an indicator of all the problems and deficiencies of the national economy. Miners formed the largest single numerical group among the unemployed, though the rate of unemployment (excluding short time) was only just above the national average. Real wages fell more drastically between 1920 and 1924 than in most trades elsewhere. (Phillips 1976: 23)

By 1925, half of Britain's miners worked in collieries that had started work before 1875. International forces also worked against the interest of the coal miners. The Versailles peace treaty required Germany to supply free reparations of coal to its former enemies, Italy and France (Phillips 1976: 25–26). In response to the demands of the owners of the coal mines, the British labor movement was strong enough to mount a general strike. Together with the other consequences of the return to the gold standard, the general strike toppled the government, but neither the mines nor the miners ever regained their Victorian glories.

The experience of the coal mine strife and the general strike that followed it provided a harsh lesson to those who were willing to learn from it. The events leading up to the General Strike amply demonstrate the human costs of trying to make the economy conform to the abstract rules of the market. Churchill himself seems to have realized the folly of his policy. In a 1927 letter to Sir Richard Hopkins, a high-ranking Treasury official, he wrote:

> The comfortable [Treasury Department] attitude of letting everything smash into bankruptcy and unemployment in order that reconstruction can be built up upon the ruins, is neither sound policy nor wise economics. . . . This comfortable Victorian doctrine may have the consequences of throwing scores of thousands of men out of employment and leading to immense expenditures in other directions. What is airily called 'cutting out dead

> wood' means transferring vast masses of workmen and their families from productive industry into Poor Law. . . . I should think on the whole with 300,000 miners unemployed we have cut out enough dead wood for the moment. (Churchill 1927: 1310)

The gold standard was an especially unforgiving master. Indeed, Peter Temin has recently made the case that the Great Depression as a whole was an almost inevitable result of a policy of responding to the economic shock of World War I with an attempt to return to the austere dictates of the gold standard (Temin 1989). In this sense, Keynes' warning in 1923 that "the fluctuations in the value of money since 1914 have been on a scale so vast as to constitute . . . one of the most significant events in the economic history of the modern world" does not seem so farfetched. The eventual departure from the gold standard offers further evidence that the market just does not adjust very well.

Unfortunately, the lesson of the General Strike was lost on most conventional economists. They tend to explain the existence of any economic difficulty as conclusive evidence that some impediment to the market was at work.

Another Glimpse at Keynes' General Theory and Instability

Let me begin this section by reviewing some of our earlier discussion. While I earlier made the case that Keynes' *General Theory* was a study of stability rather than instability, one can find a glimmering of analysis of instability there. Keynes would have agreed with Adam Smith that "the establishment of any new manufacture, of any new branch of commerce . . . is always a speculation." With any speculation, what Samuel Johnson referred to as "the *Potentiality* of growing rich beyond the dreams of avarice" may prove chimerical.

While some investments do fail and others prosper wildly, for the most part, investments are reasonably stable enough that we are surprised when crises occur and investment failures become commonplace. What, then, keeps investment values from flying all over the place? Keynes attributed this relative stability to the inertia in psychological moods. I also claim that Keynes did not go particularly far in analyzing this psychological stability.

Keynes, however, did point to one specific factor that tended to reinforce this tendency toward stability, namely, the stability of money wage. We will return to this matter in more detail later in Chapter 9. I will make the case that institutions, customs, and practices, such as those that tend to keep wages stable, serve an essential purpose in our economy. They create inertial forces that buffer the economy from the sort of dramatic instability that is common in the foreign-exchange market, a sector that has much less protection from the wild swings that are endemic to market forces.

Schumpeter

Joseph A. Schumpeter

Earlier, I mentioned that Keynes was probably the first economist that would come to mind whenever the subject of instability would arise. Until recently, most economists would have probably agreed that Keynes was the most influential economist of the twentieth century. In the past few decades, however, his influence has waned somewhat, while the reputation of his great rival, Joseph A. Schumpeter, has grown by leaps and bounds.

Schumpeter, both in his intellectual and in his personal life, defies classification. He was an ultraconservative, so much so that J. Edgar Hoover investigated him as a Nazi collaborator, yet Schumpeter's favorite students were Marxists. Schumpeter attempted to use Marx's analytical system to show that capitalism would collapse by virtue of its success. In particular, he predicted that the growing affluence of a capitalist society would create sociological changes that would ultimately lead the world to a socialist future.

Although Schumpeter was a conservative, he attacked the central vision of economics. Where most economists persist in assuming that market forces will necessarily move an economy toward an equilibrium, Schumpeter insisted that market forces naturally destroy equilibria and create instability. Where conventional economists describe how a firm adjusts to the existing system of prices, Schumpeter emphasized the role of the entrepreneur who promotes major innovations that disrupt the economy. He dramatically referred to this process as "the perennial gale of creative destruction" (Schumpeter 1950: 84, 87).

For Schumpeter, bursts of "competition [come from] the new commodity, the new technology, the new source of supply, the new type of organization . . . —competition which makes a decisive cost or quality advantage and which strikes not at the margin of profits and the outputs of existing firms, but at their very lives" (Schumpeter 1950: 84). For example, when calculators displace slide rules, the producers of slide rules have to produce another product or disappear from the scene. Schumpeter, however, had his sight set on more strategic innovations, such as when the microchips developed to replace slide rules reappeared in the computer, which then forced industry after industry to reorganize on a massive scale.

This part of Schumpeter's view puts him at loggerheads with conventional economists. Where the mainstream is intent on explaining away instability, Schumpeter welcomes it with open arms. Rather than associating instability with the collapse of prosperity, he sees it as an essential element of economic development. In fact, Schumpeter views depressions as process of restoring stability by clearing away the results of bad investments made during more prosperous times.

Wolfgang Stolper, one of Schumpeter's students, interpreted Schumpeter as having anticipated the theory of punctuated equilibrium as it applies to economics (Stolper 1994: 42–4). Stolper characterizes Schumpeter's theory as follows:

> First when evolution is rapid—both the number and kinds of elements change rapidly, and so do the "rules" by which the elements interact—we may not get a movement toward equilibrium very quickly. Moreover, the eventual move toward an ordered equilibrium may be particularly painful. But since, second, the system seems in this case particularly open to evolutionary change, this might help to understand the structural changes in an economy which are intended to deal with such violent changes, in particular institutional changes. One such institutional change that is explicit in Schumpeter deals with the increasing emergence of large-scale enterprise which will—in Schumpeter's analysis—mitigate the severity of the cycle, that is will help the adaptation process. (Stolper 1994: 43–44)

Schumpeter's Place in Economics

Schumpeter's reputation is always a source of amazement to me. Economists are notoriously intolerant of anybody whose ideas are not compatible with their own—except, apparently, in the case of Schumpeter. With Schumpeter, you find Marxists admiring this crusty conservative and conservatives adoring this economist who provocatively drew inspiration from Marx. Most surprising of all, you find economists heaping lavish praise on one of the most eloquent antagonists to their beloved concept of equilibrium economics, which is the core of conventional economic theory. Everybody, with one exception, seems to find something to love in Schumpeter's work.

While economists of all political persuasions applaud Schumpeter, few can legitimately claim to follow in his footsteps. Certainly, no other economist, with the exception of Marx, painted with as broad a brush.

In contrast to modern economists, who build abstract models in an effort to capture a few elements of the economy, Schumpeter's works had a grand vision. Such titles as *Business Cycles: A Theoretical, Historical, and Statistical Analysis of the Capitalist Process* and *Capitalism, Socialism, and Democracy* suggest the panoramic nature of his work.

The one major figure who was critical of Schumpeter was that careful assembler of data, Simon Kuznets. For Kuznets, Schumpeter's *Business Cycles* was wide in scope, including "running commentaries upon specific situations, with a wealth of allusions, incisive sidelights, references to existing literature, and theoretical suggestions" (Kuznets 1940: 105; see also Kuznets 1930b).

Yet Kuznets noted that he could not "escape the impression that . . . [the] theoretical model in its present state cannot be linked directly and clearly with statistically observed realities; that the extreme paucity of statistical analysis in the treatise is an inevitable result of the type of theoretical model adopted" (Kuznets 1940: 116).

I might also mention that although some major themes persisted in Schumpeter's works, contradictions were also abundant—none more so than the question of stability. In *Business Cycles,* Schumpeter pictured the economy as experiencing cyclical movements. Within this context, depressions were a natural phenomenon.

Depressions, for Schumpeter, were a natural phenomenon that cleansed the economic body of sick and unhealthy enterprises: "Everything that is unsound . . . shows up when prices break and credit ceases to expand. . . . Nor is it difficult to see why errors and misbehavior should be abnormally frequent in prosperity. Everyone is a great business man when prices go up, and windfall profits are easily made which obliterate the consequences of errors of judgement and worse things" (Schumpeter 1934: 13).

Schumpeter continued: "Depressions are not simply evils, which we might attempt to suppress, but . . . forms of something which has to be done, namely, adjustment to . . . change" (Schumpeter 1934: 16).

In this sense, Schumpeter proposed that business cycles are not "like tonsils, separable things that might be treated by themselves, but are, like the beat of the heart, of the essence of the organism that displays them" (Schumpeter 1939: v).

Elsewhere, Schumpeter compared an economic breakdown with "a spring cleaning, going on ruthlessly, ruining much" (Schumpeter 1941: 351).

In other words, Schumpeter turned conventional wisdom on its head. Depressions allow capitalism to enjoy stability, while prosperity—at least continual prosperity—which most economists would associate with stability, threatens the foundations of capitalism.

By the time that he wrote *Capitalism, Socialism, and Democracy,* Schumpeter was no longer emphasizing the stability of capitalism but its transitory nature. He saw the Great Depression as "catastrophic" because it disrupted the entire organization of the economy (Schumpeter 1941: 352).

No longer so optimistic about the future of the economy, in *Capitalism, Socialism, and Democracy,* Schumpeter proposed that market economies would inevitably give way to socialism, and not, as Marx believed, because of the failures of capitalism but because of its success.

Schumpeter and Equilibrium

Despite the widespread outpouring of affection for Schumpeter's work, virtually no economist follows his lead. Instead, economists continue to build simplistic models, even when they label themselves and or their models as Schumpeterian.

Schumpeter's theory of instability was far more subversive than economists recognize. When economists writing admiringly of Schumpeter's "perennial gale of creative destruction," they emphasize the adjective "creative." While they might take some passing note of the destructive part of Schumpeter's formulation, they usually treat it in a Darwinian sense: survival of the fittest implies that a few may expire, but the group becomes stronger as a result.

Schumpeter, however, was no Darwinist. He understood that the competitive process could easily spin out of control. Like a snake consuming its own tail, unrestrained competition can destroy the very basis of society unless it takes preventative measures.

Schumpeter's famous reference to creative destruction came in the context of making this very point. At the time, he was discussing safeguards that might seem to serve no other end but to keep prices high. He noted: "We must now recognize the further fact that restrictive practices . . . as far as they are effective, acquire a new significance in the perennial gale of creative destruction, a significance which they would not have in a stationary state or in a state of slow and balanced growth. . . . [I]n the process of creative destruction, restrictive practices may do much to steady the ship and alleviate temporary difficulties" (Schumpeter 1950: 87).

Schumpeter continued: "[R]estrictions . . . are . . . often unavoidable incidents, of a long run process of expansion which they protect rather than impede. There is no more of a paradox in this than there is in saying that motorcars are traveling faster than they otherwise would because they are provided with brakes" (Schumpeter 1950: 88).

So Schumpeter holds that creative destruction, though beneficial to the economy, must be held in check, lest it spin out of control. This thesis became commonplace during the devastating depression of the nineteenth century, which we will discuss in Chapter 8, but by the time Schumpeter was writing, this idea had already passed into obscurity.

Schumpeter's enormous reputation was insufficient to prevent later economists from forgetting the complexities of creative destruction. Most economists who comment on Schumpeter, by emphasizing the "creative" part of creative destruction, characterize his work as evidence in favor of laissez-faire. They ignore the fact that Schumpeter was actually arguing for restrictions on market forces lest the destructive part of creative destruction wreak havoc on the economy.

Today, a professional society for the promotion of Schumpeter studies is very active. Scores of scholars publish numerous books and articles on Schumpeter each year. Most of these works give at least some mention, if not central place, to the theory of creative destruction, yet I have not seen anybody take note of Schumpeter's recognition of the fundamental instability of a market society.

Polanyi

We have to look outside of the economics profession to find anybody that has raised deep questions of economic instability. Perhaps the best modern effort in this regard was that of Karl Polanyi, a Hungarian anthropologist who emigrated to the United States. More than a half century ago, Polanyi wrote a masterpiece entitled *The Great Transformation: The Political Origins of Our Time* (1944).

This magnificent book contended that primitive societies achieved economic stability by ordering their societies through custom and tradition. Over time, custom and tradition gradually gave way to market forces. By the nineteenth century, the most advanced market societies dared to trust their future to the market to an unheard-of degree.

At this point, Polanyi took issue with the tradition of Adam Smith. He insisted that markets have no anchor but instead take on a life of their own. People and even nature itself must necessarily adjust to the dictates of the market. While markets may promise much, they also create great dangers. In particular, the experiment with market forces culminated in a major industrial depression that rocked the late nineteenth century.

In an effort to reinvigorate their economies, the advanced capitalist nations attempted to expand their colonial footholds. They could only do so by treading on their rivals' colonial plans. Ultimately, these conflicts led to the First World War and the subsequent instabilities that disturbed Keynes so much.

Soon after the war, the major market economies fell into another depression. Even before the Great Depression, many countries tried to protect themselves against the ravages of the market. By the time the Great Depression seemed to be the likely outcome of a market economy, the major market economies turned to communist, fascist, or social democratic–New Deal policies. Each of these alternative methods of economic organization shared one common trait: they all embraced more planning and less reliance on the market.

After Polanyi published his masterwork, the need to rebuild the wartime devastation, combined with economic planning of one sort or another, allowed disparate economies, from the United States to the U.S.S.R., to prosper, so much so that many powerful interests became overconfident. Leaders of the major capitalist economies decided that prosperity was the natural state of the market and that government intervention was nothing more than a costly inconvenience.

Let us hope that this burst of overconfidence leads to less mayhem than its counterpart during the nineteenth century.

The Market and the Saga of the Passenger Pigeon

Economists' elegant theories are incapable of capturing the pain and suffering engendered by markets run amok. Keynes' witty analysis of a depression was light-years ahead of the simplistic models that abounded in his day, but his cleverness rang hollow once we remember the human suffering that was going on around him. Unfortunately, we can only find real people in Keynes' work buried within opaque economic categories, such as deficient demand or unemployment.

By contrast, Polanyi took pains to show how markets could devour people with cruel objectivity. In this sense, he was a superior economist to those with formal training in the subject. Markets are no less destructive of nature than they are of society. Polanyi suggested as much by including nature as a fictitious commodity, but he gave less attention to that aspect of market failure.

We economists use a strange expression, *externality,* in discussing the devastation of natural resources. This term suggests that pollution and the wasting of resources is something peripheral to the operation of the market. In truth, these unwelcome consequences of economic activity seem to have been central to the process of economic growth.

Gardner Brown, an economist from the University of Washington, once wrote:

> The passenger pigeon is a marvelous case study for the economist. . . . The market price of passenger pigeons did not rise, because chicken was regarded as a close market substitute and the price of chicken remained stable during the passenger pigeon's demise. Since price did not rise to signal growing scarcity, there was no economic force inducing entrepreneurs to attempt to save the pigeon, because there was no evident economic scarcity rent to be earned. (1990: 212)

This unfortunate creature was doubly cursed by instinct and market forces. At the sound of gunshots, the frightened birds would flock together, making them an easy target for hunters.

Though passenger pigeons were hunted by New England settlers, significant commercial hunting did not begin until about 1840. By the 1860s, hunts of grand proportions became common (Tober 1981: 94). Consider just how grand these grand proportions were. James Tober, a student of Brown's, wrote:

> From Hartford, Michigan in 1869, 3 carloads per day were shipped to market for forty days, which yielded a total of 11,880,000 pigeons. Another Michigan town was reported to have shipped some 15,840,000 birds over a two-year period. From the Michigan nesting of 1874, a single railroad station is reported to have shipped 80 barrels per day, each containing from 30 to 50 dozen birds, for the length of the nesting season. Two reports from the Shelby, Michigan nesting of 1876 suggest that 350,000 and 398,000 birds were shipped per week. (Tober 1981: 95)
>
> The last major nesting occurred near Petoskey, Michigan, in the spring and summer of 1878, with an estimated total shipment of 1,500,000 dead birds and 80,352 live from Petoskey station alone. (Tober 1981: 96; citing Roney 1907: 92)

This massive slaughter soon took its toll on the passenger pigeon. According to Stephen Gould, "By 1870, birds were reproducing only in the Great Lakes region. Hunters used the newly invented telegraph to inform others about the location of dwindling populations. Perhaps the last large wild flock, some 250,000 birds, was sighted in 1896. A gaggle of hunters, alerted by telegraph, converged upon them; fewer than 10,000 birds flew away" (Gould 1993: 54). People comforted themselves by regarding the collapse of the population as a temporary phenomenon. In 1897, *Western Field and*

Stream wrote that the birds were "as liable to return at any time as unexpectedly as they went." *Forest and Stream,* in 1899, supposed that the species would "live long in the land, but never again as a bird found in enormous numbers" (Tober 1981: 94).

Soon thereafter, the passenger pigeon disappeared from the planet. The last member of the species, named Martha, died in the Cincinnati Zoo on 1 September, 1914, at the approximate age of 29 years. The tragic combination of market forces and instinct sealed its fate.

Free Market Environmentalism

How well did the price system anticipate the fate of the passenger pigeon? Recall that the price of passenger pigeons remained steady, despite its impending extinction, supposedly because of its grand competitor, the noble chicken (Tober 1973, Table 4.1: 170). I do not hold chickens responsible for the fate of the pigeon.

A higher price, of course, may have offered no protection for the fast disappearing bird. Higher prices might have only incited a more vigorous hunt for the few remaining birds. The key to the story is that prices, which are supposed to signal scarcity, do not and cannot accurately take the future into account. Even if prices could have such an anticipatory power, they would not work for resources that are not "produced" in an ordinary sense—that is, for what Polanyi described as fictitious resources. As a result, the market does not provide the necessary feedback to avoid disasters.

Let me add a brief footnote to this discussion. Some economists might wish to draw an unwarranted moral from the fate of the passenger pigeon. They would have us believe that the species would have been better off had the birds been treated as a form of private property—like the chicken, bred for slaughter rather than living wild. These so-called free-market environmentalists contend that private property rights will somehow ensure the protection of natural resources. Alas, the treatment of the privately owned forests and mines should remind us that the market offers little protection for nature.

Free market environmentalists also contend that the profit-minded entrepreneurs are so ingenious at finding new methods of production and alternative resources that we need not worry about scarcity at all. Their most cited piece of evidence was a much publicized bet that ecologist Paul Ehrlich and physicists John Harte and John Holden placed with Julian Simon, a free market economist noted for the vehemence with which he dismissed environmental concerns.

Simon wagered that the price of a basket of five metals (chromium, copper, nickel, tin, and tungsten) would fall between 1980 and 1990. The prices of all five metals had gone up between 1950 and 1975. But the prices of three of the five went down in the 1980s, in part because a recession in the first half of that decade slowed the growth of demand for industrial metals worldwide. Ironically, the doubling of world oil prices in 1979 was a prominent reason for the slower industrial growth (Ehrlich and Ehrlich 1996: 100–4).

Paul Ehrlich insisted that this bet did not validate Simon's naive idea that we need not worry about environmental limits, but in making his case, Ehrlich accepted the idea that prices are fairly good indicators of scarcity. According to Ehrlich, Simon won the bet only because extraneous factors, such as the recession, had modified the long term price trend.

The passenger pigeon tells a more worrisome tale: prices need not reflect scarcity at all. Prices may give us no warning whatsoever as we approach the brink of disaster.

CHAPTER 5

Competition in Biology and Competition in Economics

Fundamental Instability and Time

The early post–World War II period was perhaps the most stable economic episode in modern history. Economists commonly refer to it as the "Golden Age." Yet, despite the stability, changes obviously occurred. Not only did the economy grow rapidly but new products also came on the market. Populations became concentrated in regions that previously were relatively uninhabited. Sometimes, prices of some goods increased by 10 percent or more within a year. Other prices declined.

Yet amid these changes, stability appeared to be the norm for the system as a whole once the memory of the Great Depression dimmed. At the time, many people could reasonably expect to hold a position with the same company for decades. Most companies were earning healthy profits. At the time, few, if anybody at all, considered the possibility of pervasive instability.

Unfortunately, the presumed stability of this period was highly unusual. A longer look at history shows that massive depressions do occur, about once every half century. This pattern of apparent stability within a larger form of instability is not unique to markets. For example, astronomers teach us that the planets of the universe move in a fairly regular pattern. Somehow, the centrifugal force of a planet's momentum and the centripetal force of gravity more or less balance each other, resulting in more or less regular orbits.

Even planetary motion is not exactly stable. However stable this configuration might seem to be, apparent regularity does not guarantee indefinite stability. Over time, the planetary orbits shift, almost imperceptibly.

With the dislocation of any one planetary orbit, all other orbits must adjust accordingly. At some point, the cumulative effect of these small disturbances can suddenly take a dramatic turn. Gravitational forces can even spit a planet out of the solar system.

Since economic data do not display anything like the regularity of planetary motion, economic forecasts seem to resemble the work of astrologers more than astronomers. Certainly, no sane economist would dare to make predictions nearly as exact of those of a trained astronomer.

While many millennia may pass without any major astronomic disruption, economic activity is subject to more frequent upheavals. The reason for this difference between the two systems is not hard to fathom. Although the same physical laws that govern planetary systems also work within economies, other, less stable forces influence economies. Indeed, the forces that control the motion of the solar system are quite simple compared to the human behavior that determines the fate of the economy. Certainly, gravity or electromagnetism are easier to treat scientifically than psychological factors, such as investor confidence or consumer buying patterns. Great writers of fiction probably have as good a handle on human behavior as trained scientists do.

Leo Tolstoy began his epic novel *Anna Karenina* with the famous observation, "All happy families resemble one another, but each unhappy family is unhappy in its own way" (Tolstoy 1970: 1). Much the same can be said about depressions. Each depression seems unique and subject to as many interpretations as the most dysfunctional family.

The most studied depression of all time is the Great Depression of the 1930s. Its cause remains a matter of contention among economists (Whaples 1995). In fact, I can think of a more than a dozen economic explanations for this episode. Various economists have pointed to speculation, erratic monetary policies, demographics, an earlier fall in raw material prices, overproduction, underconsumption, increasing tariffs, the gold standard, and many more explanations.

Why should so many individual causes be seen as capable of triggering such a momentous event? To answer that question, I would suggest that we look at the market at a broader level of generality. If, as I believe to be the case, the market always stands poised at the edge of a precipice, even a small force can suffice to topple it over the edge. After the fall, we are left to search for the ultimate cause. Since the decisive factor can be trivial, any number of causes seem capable of setting off the crash. We would do better to look at the prior configuration of the economy balanced at the edge of the precipice than to search for the small force that eventually toppled the economy.

In fact, rather than asking what causes a depression, we might do better to consider how a market economy manages to avoid crises for extended periods. In what follows, I will make the case that the seeming stability between periods of crisis owes more to nonmarket forces than to some economic forces that might tend to create stability. I will show how competitive forces, which most economists believe to have a stabilizing influence, actually have an inherent tendency to cause crises.

The Lethal Punch of the Invisible Hand

According to the basic theorem of conventional economics, competitive pressure will naturally force firms to sell their wares at a price equal to the cost of producing one more item—what economists call, "the marginal cost." This marginal cost pricing, according to the central doctrine of conventional economics, will ensure both efficiency and equity.

Suppose you have a world in which prices do not equal marginal costs. Economists can demonstrate mathematically that if you could somehow change the world so that prices would become equal to marginal costs, the resulting economy will have the potential to produce more *utility*—an economics term that is supposed to indicate happiness—than the original economy.

Although the claim in the previous paragraph might sound hollow and unrealistic, the logic behind the claims of conventional economics is irrefutable. Well, at least it is somewhat irrefutable.

In reality, the extravagant proposition that this simple rule of marginal cost pricing will lead to the best of all possible worlds does rest on a set of assumptions that have little relationship to the real world. Tear away the assumptions, and the theory withers away.

First and foremost, the theory assumes that the world is unchanging. In addition, the theory assumes that the economy is viable; that is, that the most efficient firms can earn enough profit to survive. The first assumption is obviously wrong. The second requires some thought.

Why, then, should prices equal marginal costs? Take a moment to consider the nature of modern technology. In almost any major manufacturing industry and, perhaps, even the majority of the most important service providers, the marginal cost is small, if not trivial. Take an extreme example—computer software. The marginal cost, that is, the cost of producing another copy of a program, is virtually nothing. If a firm were to be paid its marginal cost and nothing more, it would earn nothing.

Now suppose that two companies have produced software products that are virtually identical. A customer goes to the first company, which quotes a price of $500. The company explains that it has spent millions of dollars in developing the program. The customer, unsympathetic to the corporate explanation, goes down the street to see the second company, which quotes her a similar price. She then says that she might as well buy it from the first company.

The manager knows that if the price falls much below $500, his company will not be able to recover the millions of dollars spent on creating the program. Nonetheless, the manager tells her that he wants her business, even though he will "lose money" on the deal, so he offers her a lower price. After all, to turn down $450 per program will do nothing to help recoup the investment that the company has sunk into research and development. The customer can take the $450 bid back to the first company, which by the same logic might be willing to drop the price to $400. Each company knows that so long as the price remains above the marginal cost, which is the cost of producing another copy of the program, they will earn something, even though the bulk of their original expenses may be lost.

This process illustrates the severe nature of the unchecked competitive process. Under strong competition, prices will fall toward marginal costs. The price of creating a computer program or the cost of purchasing plant and equipment—what economists call "fixed costs"—does not figure into the marginal cost of the good. Prices will fall toward marginal costs regardless of these fixed costs. If firms are not eventually able to cover their fixed costs, they will certainly fail.

Let us shift the focus to manufacturing to consider fixed costs in a bit more detail. Suppose we have an industry in which all the firms are selling their output at a price equal to marginal cost, say $100. One firm discovers a new technology that can actually eliminate half of the production costs. The new equipment that can accomplish this feat is expensive, but it reduces the need for a good share of the labor force. If the firm can cut its costs in half, then it can make an additional profit of $50 on each unit it sells at $100.

The marginal cost will be even less than the $50, which includes an allowance to cover the cost of the new equipment. Let's say that the new marginal cost is $25. In effect, much new technology converts marginal costs—in this case, the labor that the new technology replaced—into fixed costs, or the cost of the new technology.

So long as the price remains at $100, the firm makes a healthy profit, but if other firms pick up similar technology and drive prices down to $25 right away, the firm will be worse off than it was in the first place. It will only receive its marginal cost of $25 per unit, without gaining any return on the money that it had laid out on the investment. To make matters worse, the new technology has destroyed much of the value of the plant and equipment that it has replaced.

Why would the firm engage in this investment in the first place, if it is a losing proposition? If the firm believes that the rest of the industry will soon make the same investment, it will have no choice. Sooner or later, competition will drive the price too low for the firm to survive with the old technology. The firm's only hope in making its investment is that it can beat its competitors to the punch so that it can earn the extra $50 per unit before its competitors catch up with its technology.

In this environment, competitive pressures are forcing the industry to lay out a good deal of money on investment. Firms cannot recover their investment because they are earning only their marginal costs. Soon, we can expect widespread bankruptcy.

If competition causes all prices universally to fall by one-half, nothing would happen, any more than it would if prices were quoted in terms of fifty-cent pieces instead of a dollar. The problem is that all prices do not fall. Though product prices may fall by half, the price of the debt that firms owe does not fall at all. Since the prices that firms receive will not cover the fixed cost of plant and equipment, they would be unlikely to be able to service their debt.

Later, we will see in our discussion on inertia in Chapter 9, that such intense competitive pressures rarely build up due, in part, to the difficulty of gathering sufficient information. If such information were readily available, without a rapid increase in demand from somewhere, the workers that the new technology replaces will have great difficulty finding employment. Their lost wages cause a further collapse in demand. So if the sort of technological activity we have been considering for an industry were common throughout an economy, we could expect a severe depression.

In fact, we will see how the world experienced a similar situation in the late nineteenth century economy. The economy was growing, while profits were falling under the pressure of fierce competition, which was driving prices down toward marginal costs, especially in the railroad industry (see Perelman 1996, Ch. 3).

Where's the Beef

If the natural tendency of the competitive process is to lead to depressions, why don't we see depressions everywhere, all the time? To even suggest a natural tendency toward depressions today might sound ridiculous. After all, the developed world has not experienced a full-blown depression for more than a half century.

I have had to look long and hard to find support for such an idea from any respectable sources. Lester Thurow, dean of the School of Management at the Massachusetts Institute of Technology, did write:

> Left to itself, unfettered capitalism has a tendency to drift into either financial instability or monopoly. Tulip mania, the South Sea Bubble, numerous nineteenth-century financial panics, and the stock-market collapse of 1929 were all forerunners of the current mess in America's deregulated financial markets. The current consolidations in the U.S. airline industry are not unlike the great monopolistic trusts of the last half of the nineteenth century. (Thurow 1992: 18)

Unfortunately, Thurow never followed up this suggestive statement with any systematic analysis. If we go back a bit further to the late nineteenth century, economic opinion was very different. At the time, railroads were the key sector of the economy. Investment in railroads exceeded aggregate investment in manufacturing in every decade from 1850 to 1890. It was more than twice as large as aggregate investment in manufacturing from 1850 to 1880 (Sweezy 1954: 532). Until 1904, the book value of capital in the railroad industry exceeded the aggregate capital invested in the entire industrial sector (U.S. Department of Commerce 1975: 684, 735).

Given the dominant position of the railroads, you might think that the railroads would be prospering, but they were not. In part, shady financial speculators were looting the railroads and defrauding holders of common stock. In truth, a much larger problem haunted the railroads.

Since I have discussed this matter in detail elsewhere, I will only mention a few illustrative facts here (see Perelman 1996, Ch. 3). Given the high ratio of fixed to marginal cost, competition created havoc among the railroads. Reported revenue per ton mile fell from 1.88 cents in 1870 to 1.22 cents in 1880. In 1890, it had reached 0.94 cents. By 1900, it had fallen to 0.73 (Kolko 1965: 7). Ultimately, half of all the track constructed in the United States before 1900 fell into receivership. Similar pressures were also at work in the manufacturing sector.

In this environment, competition seemed to be a wasteful force. Rather than promoting efficiency, competition seemed to foster depressions. Economists, along with leaders from government and big business, were almost unanimous in believing that untrammeled competition was necessarily ruinous. They called for trusts, cartels, and monopolies to hold competition in check. For example, in 1876, Charles Francis Adams, great-grandson of President John Adams, and grandson of John Quincy Adams, who became a leading expert on the railroads, lamented the tendency for freight prices to approach marginal costs, creating widespread bankruptcy in the industry. He concluded: "in the complex development of modern life, functions are more and more developed which, in their operation, are not subject to the laws of competition or the principles of free trade, and which indeed are reduced to utter confusion within and without if abandoned to the working of those laws" (Adams 1876: 692).

To a great extent, the competitive world that so troubled these economists disappeared. A huge merger wave swept across the economy, symbolized by the 1901 merger that created U. S. Steel, capitalized at $1.4 billion, a sum equivalent to about 6.8 percent of the GNP (McCraw and Reinhardt 1989: 593). U. S. Steel was only a part of a far larger picture:

> Samuel Untermeyer [chief investigator of the Pujo Committee] had argued that Morgan, his partners and their peers at a handful of smaller banks were directors, voting trustees, or principal shareholders of corporations capitalized at $30 billion—the equivalent in proportion to the size of the economy, of $7.5 trillion today. Perhaps 40 percent of all industrial, commercial, and financial capital in the United States was in some way under the penumbra of this Morgan-centered Money Trust. (De Long 1992: 17)

According to the prevailing economic theory of that time, these great corporate consolidations were a cause for celebration. They would permit industry to become more efficient through economies of scale and the elimination of obsolete plant and equipment. In addition, in the absence of excess competition, the economy would be spared the enormous costs of recurrent depressions.

The Two Faces of Competition

To promote the popular acceptance of their theory about the dangers of competition, the leading economists of the day formed the American Economic Association, which is now the most prominent economic organization in the United States. The anticompetitive school could point with pride to the impressive performance of the industrial sector during the First World War. It could claim that the economy steered clear of any serious depression between the crest of the merger wave and the 1930s. It could have some justification in laying the blame for the Great Depression on the international economy rather than the structure of domestic industry. It might even have some grounds for attributing the Great Depression to the so-called return to normalcy of the 1920s, which marked a resurgence of policies to foster competition.

Even so, the theory of this anticompetitive school of economics was just as flawed as that of the competitive school that prevails today. Rather than improve their productive capabilities to meet the challenge of any potential competitors that might arise, the great consolidated firms typically would buy out new entrants (Lamoreaux 1985).

These giant corporations could not indefinitely buy up all of their potential competition. Smaller companies, with less capital values to protect and thus less to gain from restricting output, behaved more aggressively. They were more inclined to modernize and to expand. They ran their factories nearer to full capacity. Over time, their strategy further depleted the great consolidated firms while the challengers gained strength (Lamoreaux 1985; Stigler 1968: 108–12). This strategy of the dominant firms muted competitive pressures, thereby reducing the danger of a depression—at least in the short run.

In the longer run, although the anticompetitive school promoted policies that would supposedly ward off the threat of depression, these same policies led to an economy dominated by crippled dinosaurs. The decay of these dominant firms proceeded at an almost glacial pace. U. S. Steel retained much of its appearance of preeminence at least until the late 1960s, more than a half century after its formation. In the end, the corporate consolidations, which supposedly would protect the economy from the dangers of competition, left the economy vulnerable to a renewed burst of competition.

Modern economists have an equally one-sided view of the economy. They accept the dogma that competition is a purely constructive force. Left to itself, the economy is supposedly self-regulating. Stability is all but assured, except where outside forces interfere with the workings of the market. Like the anticompetitive school, the adherents of the competitive school of economics attribute the Great Depression to forces that would not throw their preferred theories into doubt. They fail to see that the seeming stability of the twentieth century occurred because of the weakness of competition, except during the Great Depression.

During the first half of the century, corporate consolidations limited competition. Immediately after the Second World War, industry in the United States faced virtually no competition. Its foreign competition lay in ruins. The domestic economy was flush with liquidity and hungry for the goods that were unavailable during the war. After a few decades, as international competition became more formidable and the level of effective demand had subsided, the government of the United States would step in with monetary and fiscal policy whenever the economy faltered. This strategy worked, at least till the end of the 1960s. I have told the story of this episode in more detail elsewhere (see Perelman 1993).

Over time, these same policies left the economy more vulnerable to competitive pressures. Virtually no modern economists recognize the dangers inherent in the competitive process. The American Economic Association, once the sounding board for the anticompetitive school, has now become a bastion of laissez-faire ideology. Today, we have an economy perhaps more susceptible to a depression than at any time during the century. To make matters worse, we have removed the safety nets that previously supported people during times of economic crisis.

Of course, I do not mean that a depression is imminent, only that any one of a multitude of causes can push the economy over a precipice. In addition, firms could adopt behaviors that could make a depression less likely. Admittedly, such behavior would seem to violate the logic of conventional analysis. For example, all firms could recognize the danger of aggressive pricing, and industry could refrain from adopting the destabilizing new technology for one of three possible reasons. First, all firms, knowing how destructive competition could be to their situation, might resist the new technology for fear of setting off a competitive struggle. Second, firms might actively collude to protect the value of their existing investments. Both of these possibilities were more likely when the giant consolidated firms dominated their industry. Today, they seem less probable. Finally, if technology is progressing fast enough, all firms might refuse to invest in new technology out of fear that it might be obsolete soon after it is in place.

So far, I have discussed competition in rather general terms. Now the time has come to think about the nature of competition in more detail.

The Use of Biological Metaphors

Admittedly, my perspective on competition goes against the prevailing economic doctrine. Most economists hold a sincere conviction that competition will inevitably ensure the best of all possible worlds. The more competition the better. Biological metaphors lay at the heart of their belief.

The interplay between economics and biology has a long, but shallow history. Darwin acknowledged that the early economist, Thomas Robert Malthus, inspired part of his famous theory of evolution. Since then, economists have repaid the compliment many times over (see numerous articles in Mirowski 1994).

Shortly thereafter, many wealthy people enthusiastically embraced the idea that an economy could best prosper by accepting the principle of the survival of the fittest, assuming all along that their wealth was an indication of their personal fitness.

This doctrine, popularly known as social Darwinism, seemed to give a scientific grounding to the notion of laissez-faire.

That Darwinism mutated into social Darwinism should not be surprising at all. In fact, the leading social Darwinist, Herbert Spencer, actually coined the phrase, "survival of the fittest" a decade before Darwin brought this concept to popular attention (Turner 1985: 11). Charles Darwin, in fact, explicitly credited Spencer with originating the term (Darwin 1964, Ch. 3).

Although Adam Smith's celebrated metaphor of the invisible hand predated Darwin by a century, modern economists, while giving lip service to Smith, have followed a more "Darwinian" vision. In particular, they have neglected Smith's notion of a social framework based on trust (see Smith 1759).

Even today, the belief that competitive forces offer the only hope of developing a steadily improving standard of living remains the intellectual cornerstone of most conventional economic thinking. According to the Darwinian perspective, competition will ensure that only the fittest firms will survive, and the success of these firms will somehow ensure prosperity for society.

In this spirit, Milton Friedman confidently insisted that firms that adopt practices that are "consistent with rational and informed maximization of returns . . . will prosper and acquire resources with which to expand," while other firms will eventually be driven toward material extinction (Friedman 1953a: 22). From this vantage point, modern economists draw on innumerable examples from biology to illustrate how economic competition results in the survival of the fittest.

This Darwinian theory has several obvious appeals. It has a commonsensical ring. Its emphasis on the individual rather than the group acts as a counterweight to the Marxian theory of class struggle. In addition, its commitment to gradualism gives comfort to those who enjoy the status quo (Rosenberg 1994: 587). On a deeper level, this similarity to biology seems to represent a rough proof of the validity of economic theory and even makes it seem natural. In Keynes' words: "The economists were teaching that wealth, commerce and machinery were the children of free competition—that free competition built London. But the Darwinians could go one better than that—free competition had built man. . . . The principle of survival of the fittest could be regarded as a vast generalization of . . . [conservative] economics" (Keynes 1926: 276).

To some extent, this faith in competition is justified. Obviously, some firms are incompetent by almost any standard. The competitive process will eventually cull them. Conversely, economists correctly insist that in the absence of competition, firms lack any compelling incentive to become efficient. In the splendid words of John R. Hicks, "The best of all monopoly profits is a quiet life" (Hicks 1935: 8).

Competition: Economics and Biology

We have already referred to the continuing strength of the United States Steel Corporation, despite the widespread recognition of the company's lackadaisical concern for efficiency (see Perelman 1996: 105–6, 142). *Business Week* has developed an annual ranking of the top 100 Global Industrial Firms. Twenty of the top 100 firms in 1912 were still in the top 100 of 1995 (Hannah 1998: 62). This statistic may suggest that competition creates more turbulence than it actually does. The merger of two successful firms in the list causes one of them to disappear. Of course, some of the twenty firms with a continued presence on the list may have retained a continually high degree of efficiency throughout the entire period.

Despite its superficial attractiveness, the biological analogy stands on shaky grounds. Joel Mokyr, who may have explored the biological metaphor in more detail than any other economist, observes that the subject is more complex than the simple analogy suggests. For Mokyr, "Firms are [merely] the units upon which selection occurs rather than the units that do the selecting" (Mokyr 1990b: 274) and that "invention, the emergence of a new technique, is thus equivalent to speciation, the emergence of a new species" (Mokyr 1990b: 276).

On an even more fundamental level, in economics we have no idea what "fittest" means. Just as biology texts often claim that the human race has survived because humans are fit, we must also acknowledge that rats and cockroaches are every bit as fit as we are—at least in terms of their ability to survive.

On a deeper level, we must ask in what sense does profitability equate with fitness. To begin with, this metaphor implicitly identifies people as consumers. Supposedly, competition will lower prices, making goods more affordable. The fitness metaphor ignores the possibility that firms may achieve their fitness in ways that harm us as workers or as citizens. Firms can become more profitable (fit) by reducing wages, pushing their employees harder, or forcing them into dangerous working conditions. They may also improve their profitability by carelessly spreading toxic substances or harming the environment in other ways. Should we take the creation of toxic wastes into account when we determine if the firm is fit?

The biological fitness metaphor also presumes that we are indifferent as to what the firm produces. Should we not be concerned about whether a firm sells bibles or child pornography? Each of us has a catalogue of profitable firms or industries that we might deem unfit or at least wish to see reined in. At some point, even the most libertarian-minded economist will point to necessary exceptions to the regime of laissez-faire, where society must step in to prevent some otherwise profitable businesses from continuing to operate without some sort of social controls.

Although the mindless application of biological metaphors, such as survival of the fittest, can be misleading, they can also serve a valuable purpose. When applied with caution, they can also prod economists into reconsidering some of their cherished ideas about the nature of competition. I hope to continue in that spirit.

Economics, Evolution, and Ecology

The imagery of survival of the fittest, whether in economics or biology, suggests a world in which two slightly different entities face a similar challenge, akin to a tournament of individual gladiators. Within the context of this metaphor, we do not distinguish between a person who may be fleeing a predator or a firm manufacturing a carburetor. In either case, the entity that is more efficient in performing the task at hand will survive, while the other will not. Of course, in the economic example, the inefficient producer can mutate itself into a more efficient mold and thereby escape extinction.

When we look at the economy as a whole, rather than just individual firms, we find that this metaphor runs into serious problems. Consider the shrinking world of the honeybee. Some time ago, a researcher in Brazil, experimenting with African bees, accidentally released a colony. Since then, these bees have been multiplying and moving north. They can easily displace their North American counterparts. From that perspective, we would have to judge them to be more fit. Unfortunately, these African bees are not nearly as good at pollinating as our imported European bees are. In addition, the African bees are more prone to attack humans. To make matters worse, their sting is far more harmful. The European honey bees are also vulnerable to pesticides, which present an even greater threat than the African bees.

Are we to conclude that the European honeybee is less fit? Or are we human beings less fit because of what we have done to the environment of the honeybee? Then again, we would be wrong to think of our actions as destroying the "natural" environment of the honeybee since the insect with which we are familiar is not native but of European origin.

Of course, we could treat the definition of fitness as elastic. For example, we could widen our definition of fitness to include resistance to pesticides. Unfortunately, changing the meaning of fitness can be problematical. Would we regard our susceptibility to pesticide poisoning to mean that we are less fit? Or should we consider ourselves to have become less fit since the African bee has made us more susceptible to death from bee stings? In addition, since much of our food supply depends on the work of specialized pollinators such as the humble honeybee, our ability to feed ourselves may eventually be at risk. Does this possibility constitute evidence of a lack of fitness on our part?

The example of the honeybee suggests that we need to look at the entire ecology of a system to understand what fitness means. In the same sense, the individualistic search for profits may produce less-than-optimal outcomes for society as a whole.

Just consider the enormous quantity of resources consumed in unproductive activities that aid in the pursuit of profits. Advertising is a common example. While some advertising provides useful information, much is misleading or downright dishonest. Diverting resources from such activities to more productive uses might give the economy an enormous lift. How does such dissipation of resources reflect on our evaluation of fitness? The early anticompetitive school thought that the elimination of wasteful sales efforts would provide great dividends for society as a whole. According to the economists of this persuasion, competition led the economy away from a position of efficiency.

Even if we ignore the complication of wasteful activities, such as advertising, we are still far from being able to make the claim that competition necessarily promotes efficiency. Suppose that we grant that competition could cull those firms that are less efficient today. Does the apparent survival of the fittest in a competitive economy necessarily mean that the surviving firms are most efficient?

I think not. Some firms may be ahead of their time. If they are given the space to develop, they might make a significant contribution, even though they might be unprofitable at this moment. The competitive process cannot necessarily distinguish such firms from economic detritus. The extinction of these promising firms works to the detriment of society.

Finally, a phenomenon that economists call "path dependence" creates another serious problem for the simple Darwinian understanding of the economy. If evolution were an automatic device for determining the best outcomes, a small accident, one that might nudge the evolutionary process in one direction or another, should have no effects over a long period. According to the theory of path dependence, such perturbations of the system can indeed over time create large cumulative effects.

The format of VCRs is a common but not universally accepted example. Sony's Betamax was supposedly a superior technology, but because the producers of the competing VHS technology were able to deliver more products to the market, VHS became the standard. In the process, Betamax, a superior technology, disappeared from the market (Cusumano, Mylonadis, and Rosenbloom 1992; for a different perspective, see Liebowitz and Margolis 1995).

Two Kinds of Laissez-Faire

In one sense, the idea that economics would appeal to biology is ironic. The basic idea of laissez-faire rests on the unproven proposition that the market is such a natural institution that anything that might interfere with its operations is certain to do grievous harm. This assertion bears considerable similarity to the dire warnings of the ecology movement, with one major difference: For the ecology movement, nature itself rather than the market is natural. Any attempt to manipulate nature will certainly end up badly.

Both the ecology movement and the free marketeers implicitly rest their respective positions on the unquestioned faith that natural processes, without outside interference, somehow inevitably lead to optimal outcomes. Despite the underlying similarity of their logic, their policy recommendations are diametrically opposed.

The reason for the difference is self-evident. For the one group, nature is nothing more than an economic resource, just waiting to be exploited; for the other, nature has a value far in excess of most mundane commercial objectives. For ecologists, humans are unwelcome intruders into nature, whose influence is often compared to a cancer in the human body. For free marketeers, in contrast, human activity, especially entrepreneurial activity, is the most important part of nature.

For free marketeers, everything is seen through the lens of money. Within this perspective, time is discounted, meaning that something today is worth considerably more than the same thing a year from now, generally on the order of 10 percent to 20 percent. In contrast, for environmentalists, values are timeless. A forest tomorrow is just as valuable as a forest today.

From an economistic perspective, because of discounting, the time frame is exceedingly short. What happens twenty or thirty years in the future is of little consequence. In a sense, the short time frame is ironic. After all, economics insists on the virtue of patience, because profits on investment represent, at least in part, the rewards for deferring consumption. In truth, economics is overly impatient, since business demands repayment for its investment within a few years; for ecologists, the time frame is much longer, even timeless.

As a practical matter, ecologists do not hold to an infinite time frame. Or better yet, we might say that ecologists often have two time frames, one prospective and one historical. The prospective time frame often projects disasters that are expected to arrive within a generation; in contrast, their historical time frame is often measured in millennia.

In the end, we are left with two perspectives of the world—the economic and the ecological. From either perspective, the role of those who hold the other view seem sacrilegious.

Punctuated Equilibria

Despite their limitations, biological-economic metaphors spill over into everyday speech. For example, we sometimes refer to old, outdated industries as "dinosaurs." According to this metaphor, the dinosaurs, which once ruled the world, passed into oblivion because more fit creatures evolved, which made the dinosaurs "obsolete," but we must take this metaphor with more than a token grain of salt. In fact, dinosaurs were probably very fit in their day. They ruled the landscape because they had an appropriate set of capabilities that allowed them to flourish within their environment.

Why, then, did the dinosaurs disappear? Their extinction probably had nothing at all to do with an ability to function in their "natural habitat." Most scientists agree that the dinosaurs fell victim to a global environmental catastrophe. Apparently, a giant asteroid crashed into the earth, suddenly setting off a process of massive environmental change. The same properties that enabled these creatures to thrive before may well have suddenly become obstacles to their future survival. Now, the once-fit dinosaurs exist only in our fossil records—except, perhaps, in the form of birds.

One school of modern biology suggests that recurring catastrophes, such as those that doomed the dinosaur, may have played a decisive role in evolution. While the traditional imagery of biological competition is one of steady, gradual improvement, this school has abandoned that perspective. It holds that evolution may be stalled or move at an imperceptible pace over long periods, measured in millennia. During such epochs, some species are always falling into extinction while the survivors become increasingly specialized by taking advantage of their existing environment. However, the pace of these changes is relatively slow.

Eventually, some catastrophic event causes a profound change in the environment. Then, during a relatively short period, great bursts of evolutionary activity take place. The rate of extinction accelerates. Much of all evolutionary change is concentrated in these brief periods. Biologists call this pattern "punctuated equilibrium." A few economists recognize that punctuated equilibrium may be an appropriate model for the economy (Mokyr 1990a; Gowdy 1993).

Specialization and Survival

So far, the story of punctuated equilibrium sounds somewhat familiar, except for the irregularity of the pace of evolution. According to the theory of punctuated equilibrium, the era of gradual evolution comes to a sudden halt with a catastrophic period of rapid and widespread extinctions.

The earth has witnessed five periods of mass extinctions (Leakey and Lewin 1995). Following each of these periods comes a time of explosive proliferation of entirely new life forms. Then the system settles down to another leisurely period in which most species gradually fall into extinction, while the remaining ones become more specialized to the new environment. Finally, the system settles into a period of relative stability.

While the story of punctuated equilibrium bears some resemblance to the conventional story of evolution, marked differences remain, especially with respect to fitness. We generally think of evolution during the long period of refinement as a delicate process of adoption to minute opportunities. As a result, within this framework more recent species, such as our own, should be more complex and more elaborate than more ancient ones.

The theory of punctuated equilibria rejects this perspective. In Stephen Gould's words: "The history of life is a story of massive removal followed by differentiation within a few surviving stocks, not the conventional tale of steadily increasing excellence, complexity, and diversity" (Gould 1989: 25; see also Gould 1994).

Biologists of all stripes acknowledge the amazing ability of various plants and animals to adapt to specialized niches. For example, scientists have recently discovered a new species, wholly unrelated to any previously known species, which survives on the lips of one particular type of lobster (Morris 1995). Although this form of evolution is remarkable, it also leaves the creatures vulnerable to even a slight change in the environment. The same specialization that made these creatures so dependent on the success of a relatively small group of lobsters makes them less adaptable to relatively small changes in the global environment. For example, this particular group of lobsters may decline or migrate to a less desirable location, threatening the existence of their tiny lip dwellers.

The recurrence of the mass extinctions suggests that many life forms may well be following paths that are not sustainable in the long run. Perhaps like the dinosaur, they may be fit, even ideally suited for their environment, but they lack the flexibility to adapt to the conditions that might follow some significant global change.

Of course, we can consider flexibility to be an important aspect of fitness, but evolution seems to be unkind to most "generalists." Specialists seem to be able to outcompete the generalists during "normal times." However, once massive changes are underway, flexibility proves advantageous. For this reason, Gould speculated that during the Jurassic age the future belonged to some of the more humble denizens of the dinosaur world:

> Perhaps the grim reaper works during brief episodes of mass extinction, provoked by unpredictable environmental catastrophes. Groups may prevail or die for reasons that bear no relationship to the Darwinian basis of success in normal times. Even if fishes hone their adaptations to peaks of aquatic perfection, they will all die if the ponds dry up. But grubby old Buster the Lungfish, former laughingstock of the piscine priesthood, may pull through. (Gould 1989: 40)

Gould's example also illustrates how evolution can lead a population along the wrong track in an unstable world. Had a biologist been monitoring the evolutionary process at the time, an extinction of the lungfish might well have gone unnoticed. Presumably, many other seemingly unfit plants and animals that became extinct with the dinosaurs might have proven to be extraordinarily fit, had they been able to survive long enough to compete under the new conditions. Instead, the relentless quest for survival let these genetic experiments expire.

Given that the earth has experienced several mass extinctions, we cannot say with assurance that the struggle for survival leads to the survival of the fittest. In part, the efficiency of the competitive mechanism depends on the frequency of the mass extinctions compared to the rate of evolution of the plants and animals during the relatively stable periods; that is, if massive disturbances in the environment occur too frequently, evolutionary adaptation could be too slow to show much positive effect.

Baseball

Gould uses baseball statistics to illustrate his understanding of the evolutionary process. Evolution in a simple game such as baseball is both fairly rapid and very familiar to a large number of people.

His data indicate that in earlier times, the variation in batting, pitching, and fielding was far greater than today. Gould's favorite example is the incidence of batting averages in excess of 400. From the earliest recorded baseball statistics until 1941, someone would achieve that level every few years, but after 1941, nobody ever again batted 400. According to Gould:

> Shrinking variation in batting averages must record general improvement of play (including hitting, of course) for two reasons—the first (expressed in terms of the history of institutions) because systems manned by best performers in competition, and working under the same rules through time, slowly discover optimal procedures and reduce their variation as all personnel learn and master the best ways; the second (expressed in terms of performers and human limits) because the mean moves toward the wall, thus leaving less space for the spread of variation. (Gould 1996: 127–8)

Gould proposes that during the first 50 or so years of baseball, the game was still evolving. People were still developing new techniques. As the game evolved to the point at which players developed a fuller understanding of the game and individuals specialized in particular roles, the scope for someone to achieve a 400 batting average narrowed and then disappeared.

The history of the Kentucky Derby tells a similar tale. Aristedes won the first race in 1875 with a time of 2:37 ¾. By 1896, the winning time had fallen to 2:07 ¾. From that point on, not much progress occurred, except in 1973, when Secretariat broke the two-minute barrier with a time of 1:59 ⅖. No horse since has ever matched that feat.

We might think of our game of baseball as comparable to the contest between predator and prey in nature. In both baseball and the natural environment, both sides have evolved specialized offenses and defenses to the point that neither can gain much of an additional advantage over the other within the existing environment.

Football is both newer than baseball and more complicated. Thus, new strategies continue to evolve. For example, the San Francisco football team built its offense around very short, very high-percentage passes, where the typical offense primarily ran the ball with the occasional long pass play. Very quickly, San Francisco began to dominate the league. Other teams responded by hiring assistant coaches from San Francisco and adopting the San Francisco offense. As a result, San Francisco's advantage disappeared.

Suppose, however, that the environment suddenly changes. For example, imagine that the rules of baseball would mutate overnight to resemble the rules of football or professional wrestling. Suddenly, the finely honed skill of laying down a bunt or converting a double play would have no value at all. Strength rather than hand-eye coordination would determine a player's ability to excel.

Evolution, of course, is far more complex than a simple game such as baseball, but here again Gould has something to tell us about competition, as well as evolution.

CHAPTER 6

Competition: The Hidden Costs of the Invisible Hand

Hopeful Monsters and Entrepreneurial Alertness

Punctuated equilibrium tells the story of evolution within an entire ecosystem. Gould proposes a different sort of account to explain how evolution might proceed within a particular species. This part of Gould's vision has some striking parallels with the perspective of some economists.

Gould picks up the story from the often-maligned Richard Goldschmidt (1940). From his study of fossil records, Gould contends that stasis, a relatively unchanging condition, is common. Of course, change occurs, but at a very slow pace. In addition, most species exhibit no directional change during their tenure on earth. They appear in the fossil record looking much the same when they disappeared. Morphological change is therefore usually limited and directionless (Gould 1977a).

Gould speculates that a species does not arise gradually by the steady transformation of its ancestors; it appears fully formed (1977a). Gould does not deny that some gradual evolution occurs within a species. Darwin showed quite conclusively that the shape of a birds' beak will certainly evolve over time according to the type of food supply that is available.

Gould is referring to morphological change through which basic structural changes in the species occur. In other words, our ancestral rodents did not merely evolve gradually until they emerged as bipeds with opposable thumbs. Instead, they bred a slew of "hopeful monsters," most of which expired without much consequence. A select few, however, survived, giving rise to entirely new species. Gould gives the example of a particular snake whose maxillary bone is broken in two with a joint. He says that no small evolutionary stages could explain such an evolutionary outcome (Gould 1977b). Instead, a freak snake must have been born with a weird feature that gave it an evolutionary advantage.

The difference between Gould's depiction of hopeful monsters and the conventional story of evolution might not seem to be very significant. In both cases, changes occur, and those species that have an evolutionary edge are more likely to survive. However, in the case of traditional evolution, the steps are small, perhaps even imperceptible. Small changes in one species might promote a different set of small changes in other species. As a result, we should expect to see the evolutionary process as gradual.

In contrast, with the emergence of a sequence of hopeful monsters, evolutionary change will become more problematical. Let us return to that strange creature that dwells on the lobster's lip. Should a new monster lobster displace the existing lobsters, the lip might no longer be a suitable abode. In retrospect, we would have to conclude that the evolution of this unfortunate creature has gone in the wrong direction. Thus, evolution could appear to move more chaotically than the traditional story would have us believe.

Even so, according to the theory of punctuated equilibrium, during normal times the pace of evolution is slow. Presumably, monsters would be rare and hopeful monsters rarer still. During turbulent times, monsters would still be rare, but the new conditions would increase the probability that a monster would be well adapted to the new conditions.

I tend to think of serendipitous technologies as an analogue of hopeful monsters. In one famous example, 3M researchers were working on an adhesive that was too weak. Another researcher, Art Fry, was frustrated because his paper book markers kept falling out of his church hymnal. He realized that the lack of strength of the adhesive could be put to good use, leading to the development of the ubiquitous Post-it note.

This story illustrates a major difference between biological and economic evolution. Imagine that the Post-it note had been a new biological species, based on an entirely different concept than other types of adhesives, the survival of which depends on their strong gripping power. As a biological entity, the Post-it note would have hopped out of the laboratory on its own. As an economic innovation, it required someone who happened to be alert to its economic viability. Had it not been for Art Fry, the weak adhesive would have been nothing more than another failed attempt to develop a new product.

Indeed, the history of technology is riddled with stories of accidents and even mistakes (the technological equivalent of hopeful monsters) that have proved to be essential in the development of various technologies. Schumpeter stressed that the key to economic development is such entrepreneurial ingenuity—the ability to see possibility where others have overlooked it. The late Nicholas Georgescu-Roegen noted the connection between Schumpeter and Gould's treatment of Goldschmidt's hopeful monsters. In Georgescu-Roegen's words: "To gauge the depth of Schumpeter's vision we should note that the explanation of speciation by successful monsters has recently been revived by one of the greatest minds in contemporary biology, Stephen Jay Gould" (Georgescu-Roegen 1990: 232).

Georgescu-Roegen reminded his readers of Schumpeter's understanding of the crucial role of discontinuity in the process of economic development. To bring his point home, Georgescu-Roegen suggested that "a railway engine is a successful monster in comparison to a mail coach" (Georgescu-Roegen: 232), alluding to Schumpeter's famous dictum, "Add successively as many mail coaches as you please, you will never get a railway thereby" (Schumpeter 1961: 64 fn; and Schumpeter 1935: 4).

Schumpeter's vision of discontinuity is largely forgotten today. Although many economists pay lip service to Schumpeter, his grandiose vision of discontinuity has largely fallen from view. The adherents of the Austrian school of economics continue to follow in Schumpeter's footsteps insofar as they emphasize the importance of entrepreneurial alertness. In reading their works, I get the impression that their understanding of alertness does not refer to the introduction of technologies that can change the entire economic landscape, such as the railroad. Instead, I get the feeling that they have a much smaller scale of alertness in mind through which entrepreneurs take modest advantage of economies that are already on hand.

I may be giving the Austrians too little credit in this regard. I should add that I appreciate how the Austrian economists have placed human creativity at the center of our hopes for creating a better world. Even so, here again, I read the Austrians as having a limited vision. They limit their praise of alertness to those who organize the workplace in an effort to explain the high rewards that accrue to employers relative to their employees. In truth, our world would fare far better if we were to arrange society in a less hierarchical fashion so that we would be able to encourage and reward alertness on the part of everybody, rather than having a small number of people giving orders to the majority.

The Evolution of the Automobile

Industry seems to develop according to a pattern similar to the model of punctuated equilibrium. An immature industry typically has many different producers and a wide variety of products. Over time, the industry settles on a more or less dominant design, which evolves relatively slowly (Abernathy and Utterback 1978).

Consider the case of automobiles. By 1908, more than 500 companies had entered the automobile industry (Flink 1975: 42; and Kolko 1963: 43). By some accounts, well over 2,000 firms had entered the industry by 1920 (Klepper and Simons 1997: 387).

During the early years of the automobile, the industry was experimenting with a variety of possible technologies. For example, in 1900, steam and electric vehicles accounted for "about three fourths of the four thousand automobiles estimated to have been produced by fifty-seven American firms" (Freeman and Soete 1982: 71; citing Klein 1977: 91).

At first, the steam engine seemed to have the inside track. Steam is less efficient than gasoline because the combustion is an indirect source of energy. Steam, however, requires less engineering because it does not use a gearbox. Steam was more popular in the United States than elsewhere, since the United States had fewer skilled mechanics at the time and cheaper energy (Foreman-Peck 1996). One observer at the time concluded that "unless the objectionable features of the petrol carriage can be removed, it is bound to be driven from the road by its less objectionable rival, the steam-driven vehicle of the day" (Fletcher 1904; cited in Arthur 1989: 126).

A recent historian of the fate of the steam car observed:

> The principal factor responsible for the demise of the steam car was neither technical drawbacks nor a conspiracy of hostile interests, but rather the fact that its fate was left in the hands of small manufacturers.
>
> It cannot be argued with confidence that the final adoption of the internal combustion engine as the standard engine for use in private automobiles was solely or even principally the result of its inherent superiority as a form of motive power. More likely it was the result of the fact that these automotive engineers who decided to adopt the internal combustion engine decided also to introduce at the same time a series of radical innovations in production engineering and in distribution. In this case at least the relative success of the rival innovations depended as much upon the managerial abilities of the entrepreneurs responsible as upon the technical merits of the alternative forms of power. (McLaughlin 1967: 271–2)

While the industry was settling on the internal combustion engine as the dominant design, a larger scale of production became possible, allowing for significant economies and foreclosing all alternative paths. For example, the price of a Model T Ford fell from $850 in 1908 to $360 in 1916, sales increased by a factor of 50, and market share increased from 10 percent in 1909 to 60 percent in 1921 (Freeman and Soete 1982: 71). As a result, more and more companies fell by the wayside. By 1926, only 59 companies remained in the industry (Kolko 1963: 43).

With the standardization in industrial design, the automobile industry followed the same course as the sport of baseball, in a twofold sense. Like the techniques of playing baseball, car design became increasingly standardized.

In addition, the car industry began to resemble the organization of major league baseball in another sense. While the game of baseball is competitive, the modern business of baseball is not. Baseball owners decide how many teams the organization will support. They share revenues, lest baseball experience a winnowing out of the weaker teams. Once the United States automobile industry consisted of a handful of large producers, they behaved not terribly dissimilarly from the major league baseball owners. Although they could not forbid others from competing, they used their powers to bully other firms to hinder other industrialists, such as Henry Kaiser, from entering the industry. In effect, by their coordinated pricing policy, they shared revenue.

In a sense, the evolution of the early automobile industry more resembles another tale of Gould's—the history of the Burgess Shale, where paleontologists discovered the proliferation of life forms that emerged during the so-called Cambrian explosion of 530 million years ago when a proliferation of new life forms emerged (Gould 1989). Over time, evolution eliminated the vast majority of these experiments, while the surviving species adapted to differing niches.

At the end of the Permian period, 225 million years ago, a spectacular catastrophe wiped out as many as 96 percent of all marine species. During the spurt of evolution that followed this mass extinction, relatively no new phyla and only a few new classes of life emerged. Instead, this period witnessed the widespread innovations based on existing life forms (Leakey and Lewin 1995: 28–29). We might compare this sort of variety to the proliferation of choices of colors or accessories in the automobile market that appeared after the industry had settled on a basic design.

The Penalty for Having Been Thrown into the Lead

In the literature of economics, evolutionary analogies generally shift between the evolution of firms and the evolution of specific products, such as the automobile. In analyzing the nature of instability, we need to pay some attention to the economy as a whole.

In 1915, Thorstein Veblen made the case that something like a post-Permian deceleration of evolution occurred for an entire economy. Veblen proposed that the German economy was able to surpass the English economy because the British built their economy around early technologies. He charged that the British rail gauges were too narrow and that the layout of the old English towns were ill suited to the transportation needs of a modern industrial system (Veblen 1915: 130–1). In addition, later economists would note that high investment in steam and gas inhibited British use of electrification (Levine 1967: 123–4). As a result, the British were "paying the penalty for having been thrown into the lead and so having shown the way" (Veblen 1915: 132).

A decade and a half later, Leon Trotsky returned to the subject of German economic achievements. For Trotsky, the very backwardness of the economies of Germany and the United States was an advantage that allowed those countries to leapfrog Britain (Trotsky 1932: 3). Again, in the 1960s, when modernization seemed to be within the reach of the colonial regions of Asia, Latin America, and Africa, Alexander Gerschenkron revived Veblen's theory, suggesting that with the proper institutional framework, backward economies could enjoy a rapid economic development (Gerschenkron 1962). More recently, Alice Amsden suggested that the success of the countries of East Asia during the 1970s and 1980s was due in part to the advantages of late development (Amsden 1989).

This literature contains two parallel threads. The first suggests that backward economies can make rapid progress by imitating the leaders. Veblen's idea that past investment can prove to be a handicap was common to the first thread. The second thread is more relevant here. It contends that leading countries get bogged down by their own past achievements. It often reflects a judgement that the leading countries get "fat and lazy." Over time, the first thread tended to recede relative to the second.

The first thread might have more appeal because the idea that previous investment could be an obstacle seems to defy economic logic. If capital goods are not productive, you can discard them or just sell them as scrap. How could the ownership of capital goods be a disadvantage?

Veblen suggested the answer. He referred to the modern industrial system as "a system of interlocking mechanical processes" (Veblen 1921: 52). Modern economists would be more inclined to use the expression "network effect." A company will not replace old locomotives, unless the rails are compatible with the modern models. Companies will resist scrapping their old, narrow gauge rails so long as most of the trains are designed to run on the existing rails. In effect, economies cannot easily mutate into hopeful monsters.

This problem of having to get many parts of the economy to change all at once casts some light on the rapid recovery of Europe and Japan after the devastation of World War II. I recall that when the U. S. balance of payments position deteriorated in the face of exports from these areas, people commonly explained that these regions had a more modern capital stock than the United States. A Japanese economist made a similar point: "Japan is an example of a fantastically creative response to defeat. . . . The defeat in the last war brought about, of course, a far greater scale of devastation in the economy of Japan, necessitating a fresh renovating start in almost every aspect" (Tsuru 1993: 67).

In effect, the war acted like a mass extinction that allowed for a new spurt of industrial evolution. It cleared away economic blockages in a way that market competition could not.

The Life Cycle of Economic Organizations

To continue with the discussion of the evolution of entire economies, I will drop the evolutionary analogy for the moment and return to the metaphor of baseball. Economies seem to fit the baseball metaphor better than industries do.

Business practices develop a degree of uniformity. Like a competitive baseball team, businesses tend to adopt basic designs of organization—"a way of doing business." Instead of elaborating strategies and techniques for scoring runs while preventing one's opponent from doing the same, firms attempt to emulate their most successful competitors (Nelson and Winter 1982: 11). As a result, a particular style of management becomes the norm.

Along with the prevailing management style, economies develop a legal structure, a system of labor organizations, and a host of other arrangements. David Gordon, Richard Edwards, and Michael Reich refer to this entire complex as the "social structure of accumulation" (Gordon, Edwards, and Reich 1982). Of course, the social structure of accumulation is nearly not as well defined as the rules of a sport. In addition, some industries will adopt the new management style before others do so. Furthermore, although the way of doing business is never entirely the same from year to year, this evolution does not proceed smoothly. In some periods, little change is apparent. In others, change is extraordinarily rapid.

A particular business might adapt quite well to a particular social structure of accumulation, only to be unable to compete once conditions change. In effect, the very characteristics that make it prosper at one time may spell its downfall at a later time. For example, Henry Ford's personality, which led him to offer to sell cars in any color so long as they were black, was suited for his time. Later, as the market for automobiles evolved, General Motors racked up huge profits by marketing a wide array of styles, while Ford's unchanged attitude almost drove the company to bankruptcy. In the words of Alfred Sloan, president of General Motors between 1921 and 1954: "Mr. Ford, who had so many brilliant insights in earlier years, seemed never to understand how completely the market had changed. . . . Mr. Ford in the 1920s . . . stayed too long with his old and once dominantly successful concept of the business" (Sloan 1964: 163 and 437).

Ironically, at an even later period, General Motors lost considerable profits to Japanese companies, which economized, in part, by narrowing their product choices.

Competition and Economic Catastrophes

According to Gordon, Edwards, and Reich, each social structure of accumulation seems to have a lifetime of about half a century. Severe depressions seem to trigger the demise of these social structures of accumulation and pave the way for the creation of new ones. The rise and fall of these social structures of accumulation creates a scenario similar to the story of punctuated equilibrium.

Few economists have absorbed the theory of punctuated equilibrium, however, instead they stubbornly adhere to their traditional imagery of competition as somehow driving a steady evolution of economic progress, all the while guaranteeing the fitness of the survivors.

Perhaps on one level this resistance is rational. Yes, catastrophes of mass extinction occur in the natural world but only on a scale of geological time. A meteor might crash into the earth tomorrow, but the probability of that event happening is so remote that we might be foolish to take it into account. Besides, the scale of such an event would be so great that nothing we do could have much effect in protecting us. So, why should we bother to concern ourselves with the possibilities of such an event?

After all, we cannot very well guide our evolution to adapt to the unknown effects of an uncertain catastrophe. Thousands or even millions of years might pass before the next great upheaval. Besides, we do not even know the direction of that event. For example, would it make the world hotter or colder? We cannot know with certainty. In that sense, we might reasonably put our concerns about the next global catastrophe on an only slightly higher level than our worry about the realization that the sun is running out of power.

But what do such matters have to do with economics? After all, economics is not biology. Dismissing the theory of punctuated equilibrium out of hand would probably not be difficult for most economists, given that the profession is brimming with cheery overconfidence, celebrating the success with which capitalism has avoided a major worldwide depression since 1929. Economists typically presume that a massive depression is virtually impossible at this stage in our history. Why, then, should they bother with the theory of punctuated equilibrium?

Indeed, economists have good reason to find the theory of punctuated equilibrium uncongenial. We have already taken note that economists often have biological metaphors in mind when they speak about competition. Their simplistic understanding of competition certainly does not fit in well with the theory of punctuated equilibrium. In fact, the metaphor of punctuated equilibrium is incompatible with the central thesis of laissez-faire theory, which holds that competition will necessarily lead to the best of all possible worlds.

While economic theory holds to the view that economies easily adjust to an equilibrium position, history indicates otherwise. Despite our recent run of good luck, economies do have a tendency to experience relatively frequent catastrophes. The regularity of these massive crises has led some economists, such as Gordon, Edwards, and Reich, to conclude that crises almost inevitably recur about every fifty years. Whether or not crises occur with such regularity, I want to repeat that, by taking a longer view of history, the tranquil conditions conducive to gradual evolutionary progress seem to be the exception rather than the rule. In fact, the majority of past hundred years has been spent either in wars, recessions, or depressions.

Like mass extinctions, depressions and recessions wipe out substantial portions of the economy. Just as the mass extinctions were associated with climatic shifts, so too do depressions and recessions often reflect changing economic conditions. On another level, I will argue that these depressions and recessions, which we typically regard as anomalies of the economic system, represent nothing so much as an intensification of the much-admired competitive process, which supposedly lies at the heart of the capitalist system.

Let me underscore this last point. In the biological theory of punctuated equilibrium, outside forces produce catastrophes from time to time.

In contrast, in economics, competition itself produces the catastrophes. In fact, catastrophes are the likely outcome of a truly competitive economy. Putting this difference aside for the moment, the application of the theory of punctuated equilibrium in economics raises some serious questions.

We can begin with one of the most important questions, aside from those concerning equity: How can we be sure that the competitive process is not snuffing out the makings of future economic lungfish?

In what follows, I will indicate why I believe that we often have no way of knowing whether any particular firm that fails or a person who falls by the economic wayside is any less fit than the survivors.

Survival of the Fittest

The metaphor of the survival of the fittest is so ingrained that few economists give much thought about their tightly held assumption that competition somehow automatically manages to winnow out the inefficient. I cannot find much justification for this blind faith in the universality of the efficiency-enhancing properties of the competitive process.

How can we square this misperception of the competitive process with three widely accepted ideas about small firms? First, small firms form the seedbed for many, if not most important innovations, in part because large firms are generally unreceptive to new ideas (Beesley and Hamilton 1984). Even previously innovative small firms often become blinded to good ideas once they mature. Xerox represents a classic example:

> Chester Carlsson started Xerox after Kodak rejected his new idea to produce a copy machine, telling him that his copy machine would not earn very much money, and in any case, Kodak was in a different line of business. . . . Steven Jobs started Apple Computer after this same Xerox turned Jobs away, telling him that they did not think a personal computer could earn very much money, and in any case, they were in a different business. (Audretsch and Acs 1994: 174; see also Audretsch 1995: 54)

Apple, in turn, later became relatively stodgy and stumbled because it failed to introduce exciting products for a relatively long time, at least relative to the speed with which the computer industry evolves.

The second widely accepted belief concerns the effect of tight credit. When financial stringency sweeps across the economy, it annihilates the most vulnerable firms. Finally, the third belief holds that small firms are far more vulnerable to economic crises than their larger counterparts, especially because of their disadvantages in obtaining credit (see Gertler and Gilchrist 1994).

The implication of these three ideas is that depressions are likely to destroy some of the very firms that are, in a sense, best suited to survive. Of course, I do not mean that depressions perversely single out the most efficient firms while letting the inefficient prosper. On the contrary, many firms that fall by the wayside are indeed inefficient by any objective standard. My point is merely that the destructive gale of a depression does not necessarily single out those firms that are unfit. Instead, all firms that are vulnerable at the moment are at risk.

A single idea that might have come from a promising seedbed firm might save far more resources than would be consumed in sustaining a hundred admittedly inefficient firms. Unfortunately, the sort of broad-based liquidations that occur during crises do not discriminate between such seedbed firms and the dross.

Stephen Gould once compared natural selection to a hecatomb. His words also apply to a strongly competitive economy: "A hecatomb is, literally, a massive sacrifice involving the slaughter of one hundred oxen—a reference to ancient Greek and Roman practices. By extension, a hecatomb is any large slaughter perpetrated for a consequent benefit. Natural selection is a long sequence of hecatombs" (Gould 1993: 146).

In the course of an economic hecatomb, we have no reason to believe that competition necessarily serves to enhance efficiency by enforcing a regime of the survival of the fittest. True, many weak firms will succumb to competition, but as I noted above, the selection process is also likely to destroy many of the firms with the greatest productive potential for the future.

To make matters worse, depressions can actually strengthen the so-called dinosaur firms, which we might expect natural selection to target. How, then, could depressions aid the firms that would seem to be least fit to survive? The answer is the flip side of the story of the destruction of the promising small firms.

One of the few facts about which economists agree is that depressions cause the financial system to allocate a greater share of credit to larger firms than it does during more prosperous times. Although large firms may wobble a bit under the crush of a depression, by eliminating potential competitors, large firms' competitive position will be strengthened once the crisis has passed.

The purely economic damage that depressions cause go beyond the snuffing out of the seedbed firms. More and more, economists are coming to recognize the importance of long term relationships in allowing firms to operate efficiently. Firms may have long term relations with workers, suppliers, customers, and creditors. These relations may involve information about the participants, including an estimate of the others' trustworthiness, predictability, or other characteristics. A depression changes the economic terrain, wiping out much of the value of this information.

Ben Bernanke, an economist from Princeton University, has made a great deal of this phenomenon, emphasizing the breakdown in the information between banks and their customers as an explanation of how the Great Depression became so severe (Bernanke 1983). Bernanke's understanding is not very different from Schumpeter's earlier-cited observation about the disruption associated with the Great Depression, although Schumpeter did not elaborate on this idea.

Similarly, some economists have pointed to the dissolution of long term contractual relations as the main reason that the gross domestic product of the former Soviet Union has fallen so drastically with that region's turn from socialism (Blanchard and Kremer 1997). These economies fell an estimated 35 percent between 1989 and 1994, comparable to what market economies experienced during the Great Depression (Blanchard and Kremer 1997: 1091).

Punctuated Economic Equilibrium

In a sense, the theory of punctuated equilibrium presents a curious paradox for economic theory. Obviously, if competition does not create intense catastrophes, then the theory of punctuated equilibrium would be less relevant for economists; however, laissez-faire ideology will also be inapplicable.

As I previously noted, we may think of a depression as nothing more than an intensification of competitive pressures. Without strong competitive pressures, the entire rationale for laissez-faire disappears. After all, the basic idea of a free market is supposed to be that market forces effectively discipline business to become efficient.

This discipline of competition is anything but steady. The relationship between the extent of turnover among the top tier of the corporate structure provides a crude index of the degree of competition. Of course, we cannot disentangle how much of this stability represents the ongoing efficiency of the corporate leaders rather than a lack of competitive pressure.

As we saw during such periods as the postwar boom in the United States and elsewhere, when competition becomes less intense, management slackens off, becoming fat and lazy instead of lean and mean. Hence, we should not be surprised to find a high level of stability in the period following World War II. Indeed, David Audretsch reported that two decades passed before a third of the Fortune 500 was replaced, between 1950 and 1970. As competition from imports heated up, stability declined. For example, one decade was enough for the replacement of a third of the firms between 1970 and 1980. The process continued to accelerate during the next decade, between 1980 and 1990, when a third of the firms were falling from the list every five years (Audretsch 1995: 7).

This "hardening of the industrial arteries and decreased competitiveness" of industry in the United States (Caves 1977: 40, and Caves 1980: 514) began well before the postwar boom. One study compared the rate at which firms fell from the top 100 firms in the period 1903–1919, with 1919–1969. The rate of failures per one hundred firms per year was at the least three times as great in the earlier period. The author concluded: "The evidence reviewed above indicates that corporate capitalists had achieved a quite widespread and enduring consolidation of their positions by 1919" (Edwards 1975: 442). Another study found that turnover among the largest firms had already declined over 1909–29 period, just as we should expect after a period of corporate consolidation (Stonebraker 1979).

Unfortunately, beyond warning against business collusion or government intervention, conventional economics tells us nothing about why the variability of competitive pressure might allow a large number of businesses to become inefficient at one moment and then suddenly subject these same businesses to the rigors of competition soon thereafter. This variability of the process seems to have more in common with the theory of punctuated equilibrium than the ideology of laissez-faire.

In contrast to the story of the variability of competition in the previous paragraph, conventional economic theory maintains firms are always and everywhere optimizing their profits. Some firms might not quite be operating at maximal efficiency, but economic theory predicts that they will soon mend their ways or fall by the wayside. A few mainstream economists have questioned this perspective. Herbert Simon, for one, even won the Nobel Prize for economics (see Simon 1996, esp.: 28–29), although this aspect of his work probably did little to improve his standing within the profession.

Suddenly, with the onset of a depression, competition suddenly intensifies. For example, between 1929 and 1933, one third of manufacturing establishments in the United States closed; in the motor vehicle industry, which was more concentrated than the typical industry, the figure was one half (Bresnahan and Raff 1991: 317). If competition were a steady influence, we would not see a spike in plant shutdowns during depressions.

The dissident economists Gordon, Edwards, and Reich seemed to be attempting to address this variability in the strength of competition with their theory of the social structure of accumulation (Gordon, Edwards, and Reich 1982). They even provide an overview of the history of the U. S. economy in terms of the evolution of the social structures of accumulation. Their social structures of accumulation include the gamut of forces that shape the business environment.

Gordon, Edwards, and Reich explain how these structures go through a life cycle, tentatively emerging, taking shape, then hardening, and finally collapsing. Although the authors go into enormous detail about the particulars of each social structure of accumulation, they never get around to offering a full explanation of the underlying dynamics of the social structure of accumulation. Instead, crises that inexplicably arise around every half century drive their version of history. We never discover why these crises recur any more than Gould tells us why the earth experiences mass extinctions every so often.

We should expect the life cycle of the social structure of accumulation to differ from mass extinctions in one respect: As I already noted, all of the previous mass extinctions are due to forces beyond the power of any creatures on the face of this planet. All these earlier mass extinctions also predate humankind. In the case of the crises that annihilate the social structures of accumulation, human activity is responsible for the damage that occurs.

Unfortunately, while crises affect the social structure of accumulation, Gordon, Edwards, and Reich do little to explore the effect that the social structures of accumulation might have on the formation of crises. So, their work can explain a diminution of competitive pressures, but we are left in the dark about the underlying process whereby a social structure of accumulation eventually unleashes a new wave of competition.

I do not pretend to have a thorough analysis of what determines the ebb and flow of competitive forces, but I do have a suspicion: Normally, business leaders prefer to take a live and let live approach to the market. We see indications of this tendency in the perennial impulse to bureaucratize and routinize business practices. In this regard, we can also take note of the zeal with which management takes on both staff and perks during good times.

"Satisficing" or Optimizing

According to Herbert Simon, managers "satisfice" rather than optimize. The existence of "satisficing" reflects a twofold limitation of economic theory. To begin with, firms could not really optimize even if managers attempted to do so. As Simon insists: "Because real-world optimization, with or without computers, is impossible, the real economic actor is in fact a satisficer, a person who accepts 'good enough' alternatives, not because less is preferred to more but because there is no choice" (Simon 1996: 28–29).

He continues: "Many economists, Milton Friedman being perhaps the most vocal, have argued that the gap between satisfactory and best is of no great importance, hence the unrealism of the assumption that the actors optimize does not matter; others, including myself, believe that it does matter, and matters a great deal" (Simon 1996: 29).

Furthermore, satisficing has a second dimension. Even if management had the technical capacity to optimize, they would be unlikely to do so. After all, automatic calculating devices do not run firms; flesh and blood people do. These people have preferences that may not coincide with the abstract ideals of economic efficiency.

The idea of satisficing therefore suggests the idiosyncratic choices of people rather than an automatic playing out of economic forces. While Simon's distinction earned him a Nobel Prize in economics, his appeal to satisficing rather than optimizing distanced him from the profession. In the end, he retreated to the psychology department of his university, while his colleagues from Carnegie-Mellon University went on to found a now-discredited school of economics based on the extreme hypothesis that the market could foresee the future (Sent 1997).

Yet Simon was far more in touch with reality than the rest of the profession. Many business leaders take advantage of the many opportunities for free choice that lax economic pressures provide. For example, economists are well aware that management often chooses policies to increase the growth of their firms rather than maximize profit (see Marris 1964; and Jensen 1993).

A study of the history of the economy of the United States indicates that except for a few, relatively short periods, business and government have conspired to keep these competitive forces in check. The leaders of business and government had good reason to fear that heavy competition is the natural outcome of unrestrained market processes. Despite their preference for a more restrained form of competition, competitive forces eventually tend to develop a momentum of their own. As I mentioned before, these periods of intense economic pressure seem to break out around every half century. With each outbreak of intense competition, the economy falls into a depression, bringing ruin in its wake.

Admittedly, my understanding of competition runs counter to the prevailing ideas about this subject. When economists look at modern economies, they presume that competitive forces are always dominant, except in some specific cases in which government or unions interfere with the process. Recall Milton Friedman's confident claim that government is inevitably the cause of recessions and depressions. In addition, they treat the degree of competitive pressure as being relatively constant. Finally, the dominant attitude regards competition to be relatively benign in the sense that vigorous competition, along with economic growth, is considered the normal state of affairs.

According to this conception of the economy, which the popular media reflect today, competition does not appear to be particularly threatening. The market gets credit for all that is good and efficient in the economy, while governments (and perhaps unions) shoulder the blame for all the evils.

In contrast, I would argue that the government, business, as well as certain institutional arrangements combine to hold competitive forces in check. True, these restraining forces cannot work indefinitely; yet without these institutional restrictions, the economy could fall into a situation in which depressions would be the norm rather than the exception.

Harvey Leibenstein's X-Efficiency

Not all economists accepted the idea that competitive forces somehow automatically keep the economy operating at near optimal levels of performance. A number of economists observed that the real economy hardly resembled the abstraction of a perfectly competitive economy. Even the untrained observer could see that in many sectors, a few giant corporations dominated an entire industry.

Arnold Harberger, a University of Chicago economics professor who later became the president of the American Economic Association, developed the most influential effort to refute this critique of the competitive nature of the economy. He estimated that the welfare loss from the existence of monopoly in the United States was virtually nonexistent—a mere 0.07 percent (Harberger 1954). Thus, according to Harberger the allocative efficiency, or the extent to which the market allocates resources in such a way that maximizes economic efficiency, is quite high.

Harberger's estimates seemed to vindicate conventional economics. His numbers implied that even though the structure of the economy did not look like perfect competition, the outcome was virtually the same as if perfect competition had prevailed. Some economists challenged Harberger's estimates. For example, in the first edition of his influential textbook on industrial organization, Frederick Scherer estimated that monopolies imposed social costs equivalent to about 6 percent of the Gross National Product. In the 1990 edition, Scherer and his co-author declined to revise the estimate because people carelessly bandied the figure about without taking the caveats into account (Scherer and Ross 1990: 678).

Several subsequent articles did concur with Harberger's findings. Probably most economists at the time accepted Harberger's estimates as proof that something like perfect competition was at work in the economy, without the sort of reservations that Scherer offered.

A decade later, Harvey Leibenstein responded to the Harberger literature on allocative efficiency with his famous article about x-efficiency. Leibenstein coined the unusual term x-efficiency to contrast with the notion of allocative efficiency. In addition, the "x" was to signify that something unmeasurable was at work—an unknown x factor (Leibenstein 1966).

What did Leibenstein find wrong with Harberger's approach? He pointed out that Harberger based his estimates on aggregate measures. In other words, Harberger lumped many thousands of firms together to form measures for huge industrial sectors. Leibenstein contended that these aggregates masked a great deal of inefficiency, which Harberger's analysis could not possibly capture. As Schumpeter insisted: "[Aggregation] keeps the analysis on the surface of things and prevents it from penetrating into the industrial processes below, which are what really matters. It invites a mechanistic and formalistic treatment of a few isolated contour lines and attributes to aggregates a life of their own and a causal significance that they do not possess" (Schumpeter 1939: 44).

Suppose that Leibenstein were correct, that within the aggregates a great deal of x-inefficiency existed? How could inefficient plants survive if firms were engaged in a life and death struggle in which only the fittest would survive? Leibenstein's response to that question consisted of a number of examples to show that inefficiency was rampant. For example, he pointed to wide productivity differentials in nearby plants using similar technology.

In effect, then, Leibenstein insisted that economists realize that force of competition was relatively modest, that it did not require business to operate with anything like optimal efficiency. Instead, the economy allowed firms to enjoy considerable "organizational slack" (Simon 1979: 509).

In other words, Leibenstein was saying that competition was not particularly effective in keeping the economy at peak efficiency. One author later referred to the respective losses from allocational inefficiencies, unemployment, and x-inefficiencies as "fleas, rabbits and elephants" (Vanek 1989: 93; cited in Schweickart 1996: 81).

The timing of Leibenstein's article is important. Writing in 1966, Leibenstein was working from the vantage point of the final years of the postwar boom. For more than two decades, a buoyant economy had weakened the force of competitive pressures. Many "dinosaur" firms enjoyed a comfortable existence despite their well-known inefficiencies.

Within a couple of years, the postwar boom would begin to unravel. Foreign competitors would soon become strong enough to challenge the great behemoths of U.S. manufacturing. Eventually, these firms would experience severe downsizings. Deindustrialization would become a common feature of the U.S. economic landscape.

Intangibles

Recall what Stephen Gould found in his study of baseball statistics. In baseball, intense competition weeded out all but the most capable players. Baseball employs few players that consistently bat below 200. Teams casually release yesterday's hero as soon as they sense that his abilities are dropping off. Shouldn't we expect that the economy would liquidate the poor performers as efficiently as the owners of major league baseball?

Business and the game of baseball are two very different phenomena. In baseball, once a game ends, a win is a win. Everybody knows who won and who lost. Of course, the differences between the business of baseball and business in general are not nearly as great, but I am referring to the game of baseball. The business of baseball discriminated against blacks for economic reasons, even though such policies removed many capable athletes from the potential pool of players. From a business point of view, discrimination made sense because integration hurt attendance (Hanssen 1998: 617–22).

I will concentrate on the game of baseball rather than the business of baseball. In the game of baseball, winning and winning alone is what counts. Some time ago, I heard the story of Leo Durocher, famed manager of major league baseball teams, explaining why Eddie Stankey was his favorite player. Durocher told a reporter, "He can't hit; he can't run; he can't field; he can't throw. He can't do a goddam thing, Frank,—but beat you" (Durocher 1975: 13).

The story stayed with me because it is so exceptional. Sportscasters speak of players with intangibles, athletes who, like Stankey, supposedly have intangibles that give them a value that the untrained eye cannot perceive. In reality, most fans with even a passing knowledge of the game can see what each player contributes to the team. Economists have even been fairly successful in developing statistical formulae that give a rough approximation of the contribution of each player to a team's success.

Business is far less transparent. True, at the end of each business quarter, firms report profits or losses based on complex accounting procedures. Very few people are able to interpret exactly what transpired based on such records. In addition, tax considerations distort accounting records.

To make matters even more complicated, what helps or hurts profits today might have the opposite effect over the long run. If I cut research and development funds today, this quarter's profits might improve, but the long-run prospects of the firm might deteriorate.

Finally, business leaders employ skilled public relations operations, both within and outside of the firm, to tout their achievements to the public. How often do we read a torrent of stories about the magnificent accomplishments of some business leader, only to learn later he had left a company in ruins? Even after the leader has departed, we may still find differing interpretations of his role in the fiasco.

So the business world is populated by numerous would-be Eddie Stankeys; that is, people whose contributions far exceeds what they appear to be. In this environment, the forces of natural selection cannot work with precision. This environment allows for a far greater dispersion of abilities and accomplishments than the world of professional sports would ever permit.

Leibenstein's Challenge

Leibenstein's article carried a twofold challenge. In the first place, strong competitive forces were not weeding out inefficiencies, or at least they were not doing so in a timely fashion. In addition, Leibenstein's article posed some serious questions for the way that economists go about understanding the economy.

If Leibenstein were correct, the abstract models of conventional economics would seem to have little relevance. Not surprisingly, for the most part, conventional economics was hardly sympathetic to the notion of x-inefficiency. Leibenstein's obituary recalled that between 1969 and 1980, the article was the third most frequently cited in the Social Science Citation Index. However the second remarkable aspect is that much of this citation derived from attempts to explain X-efficiency theory away: it was under almost constant attack from much of the mainstream of the profession over that same dozen years. How to reconcile this tension between the profession's admission and denial of its shortcomings (Dean and Perlman 1998: 141)?

The most famous attack came from George Stigler, self-appointed "enforcer" of economic orthodoxy (Freedman 1998). Stigler caustically entitled his article, "The Xistence of X-Efficiency" (Stigler 1976). Given his typically vehement attacks on those who dared to question the conventional economic model—one admiring student likened Stigler's style to a "Demolition Derby" (Sowell 1993: 787)—the substance of Stigler's response to Leibenstein was comparatively mild. Stigler acknowledged that Leibenstein's article was "influential" (Stigler 1976: 213). He further admitted: "Waste can . . . arise . . . if the economic agent is not engaged in maximizing behavior" (Stigler 1976: 216). Rather than attacking Leibenstein head on, Stigler turned the tables on him, contending that "unless one is prepared to take the mighty methodological leap into the unknown that a nonmaximizing theory requires, waste is not a useful economic concept. Waste is error within the framework of modern economic analysis, and it will not become a useful concept until we have a theory of error" (Stigler 1976: 216).

In other words, Stigler was demanding that Leibenstein or anybody else who follows him be prepared to develop a rigorous theory of error or, equivalently, a theory of intangibles—an impossible task by any stretch of the imagination. According to Stigler, if economists are not prepared for this impossible task, then they should abandon their entire "framework of modern economic analysis."

This prospect is terrifying to a person who has gone through the difficulties of mastering the arcane mathematical theorems of economic theory. Economic theory may be simplistic, but as graduate programs in economics teach it, it is certainly not simple. All the hard work in learning this theory would be for naught.

Economists could not easily make mathematical models or perform statistical tests on Leibenstein's unseen x-factor. Rather than coasting along by assuming that everybody operates at maximum efficiency, economists would have to begin from the beginning in order to learn why people do *not* maximize. Few economists needed George Stigler to tell them what was at stake. Leibenstein continued to promote the notion of x-efficiency, but it never took hold among many economists. Aside from the articles dismissing Leibenstein's work, economists more or less conveniently forgot what he had to say.

In retrospect, we see that Leibenstein did have one option open to him. He could have responded to Stigler by noting that the degree of waste is a reflection of the extent of competitive pressures. Moreover, the fluctuations in economic pressure are of crucial importance in understanding economic performance.

Unfortunately, Leibenstein never acknowledged that the extent of x-efficiency might fluctuate. In fact, he was probably writing at a high point of x-inefficiency. Soon after his initial article, a wave of imports began accelerate competitive pressures. A ruthless wave of downsizings followed.

Leibenstein's work on x-efficiency should have put him in a position to recognize what was about to happen. Had Leibenstein been able to communicate that point, economists might have been better prepared for the wrenching adjustments that began within a decade after Stigler challenged the relevance of the concept of waste.

The Recantation of Arnold Harberger?

While an upswell in competitive pressures certainly evened out some of the differences in x-efficiencies, they did not entirely extinguish them. To make this point, we can turn back to the recent work of Arnold Harberger. In his presidential address to the American Economic Association in January 1998, Harberger never mentioned the name of Harvey Leibenstein. Nonetheless, he delivered a fascinating talk that vindicated Leibenstein in many respects. To begin with, Harberger offered specific examples of innovations that indicated the sort of wide dispersion of productivity differentials that were at the heart of Leibenstein's work:

> I recall going through a clothing plant in Central America, where the owner informed me of a 20-percent reduction in real costs, following upon his installation of background music that played as the seamstresses worked. And then there is the story of two Chilean refrigerator firms that ended up as parts of a single conglomerate at one point. The new management reduced the number of models from something like 24 to two, making agreements

> to import other models while exporting these two. The end result was that output more than doubled, while the labor force was cut to less than half, and even the capital stock (at replacement cost) was significantly reduced. This sounds like (and is really) economies of scale, but they would not be detected by our usual measures, as both labor force and capital stock went down. (Harberger 1998: 3)

Note that we also have in this single paragraph an implicit recognition of the diversity of production methods, as well as an acknowledgement that traditional measures would fail to pick up the essence of the situation. Again, Harberger's message seems to be at one with that of Leibenstein. In addition, Harberger's comparisons were almost identical to those that Leibenstein used three decades earlier.

Harberger used an extraordinary analogy, that of yeast versus mushrooms, to highlight his insights about the diversity of production methods. Harberger used the image of yeast, which causes bread to expand very evenly, like a balloon being filled with air, to suggest the traditional image of new production technologies permeating the economy evenly. In contrast, mushrooms have the habit of popping up, almost overnight, in a fashion that is not easy to predict (Harberger 1998: 4). Harberger declared himself on the side of the mushrooms, seemingly aligning himself with Leibenstein, who also found surprising differences in productivity between seemingly similar firms.

At first, Harberger seemed to veer onto a different track than Leibenstein. He reported that the top 10 percent of industries (measured by initial value added) accounted for 30 percent of total real cost reduction (RCR) in the United States for the period 1958–1967; the top 22 percent of industries accounted for more than half of total RCR (Harberger 1998: 5). In 1970–1975 the cumulative RCR of just 25 percent of manufacturing industries (measured by initial value added) was equal to the total RCR for manufacturing as a whole. Other industries producing another 40 percent of the total had gains, but their contribution was offset by the other 35 percent of industries with negative RCR during the period (Harberger 1998: 6). Harberger reports similar results for later five-year intervals.

Of course, Leibenstein was concerned with differences within industries rather than between industries. However, Harberger also looked at the dispersion of productivity growth within industries. Here again, he found support for Leibenstein's position. Harberger explicitly confessed, "Until quite recently . . . the image that I had in mind was one of yeast within each industry and mushrooms between industries" (Harberger 1998: 10). Then Harberger declared that he had come around to Leibenstein's point of view. He admitted, "I think the result is quite clear already; namely, the 'mushrooms' story prevails just as much among firms within an industry as it does among industries within a sector or broader aggregate" (Harberger 1998: 11).

As evidence, Harberger reported on a wide dispersion of productivity gains within Mexican industries, as well as the oil industry of the United States. In the latter case, he found that the cost reduction of three firms more than equaled the reduction for the entire industry (Harberger 1998: 16ff).The productivity gains and losses for the other nine firms canceled out each other.

I would be surprised if Harberger drew the same moral from his tale as I do. In truth, Harberger never responded to Leibenstein, even though Leibenstein directed his challenge at Harberger's earlier work on allocative efficiency. In that initial article, Harberger was at pains to show that the market works and that antitrust was ineffectual.

Leibenstein was not attempting to disprove either of Harberger's points about markets working well or about antitrust. Leibenstein merely wanted to show that Harberger's method from the early article could not pick up the enormous disparity of efficiencies within firms. Stigler, however, saw that Leibenstein's article did in fact undermine the theories that such people as Stigler and Harberger cherished. If x-efficiency were a major factor in the economy, then economists would have to confront new factors for which they were ill prepared.

So, in truth, Harberger never entered the debate. He gave no indication that disparities in x-efficiencies undermined the case for markets at all. In fact, he concluded his presidential address by suggesting that his evidence somehow indicated that markets work and that governments mess things up. In short, he gave his audience no reason to find any difference in his two works, despite his conversion from a believer in yeast like processes to an acceptance of mushroom like phenomena.

Rather than mentioning the possibility that x-efficiencies were at work, Harberger blamed the deficiency of the lagging firms on poor government policies that lead to inflation, bad regulation, and protectionism (Harberger 1998: 22–3). Harberger did little to explain why these government policies should create differing effects among firms. Inflation, by interfering with price signals, might make for greater variance among firms, but he never indicated how protectionism or bad regulation might have such an effect.

I draw a different lesson from the story of x-inefficiencies than either Leibenstein or Harberger. Competitive forces generally remain too weak to force firms to launch an all-out effort to wring all the x-inefficiencies out of their operations. I will make two further additions to this claim:

First, that competitive pressures fluctuate over time; second, when competitive forces build up enough momentum to reduce x-inefficiencies significantly, they threaten to collapse the entire economy into a depression.

Summing Up

Punctuated equilibrium is only a metaphor, albeit a useful one because it provides a counterweight to the gradualist vision of conventional economic theory. The underlying sense of gradualism that pervades most economic theories creates a false sense of complacency. If nothing untoward changed today, it is not likely to happen tomorrow, either.

The metaphor of punctuated equilibrium introduces an element of realism by reminding us that the foundation of our economy is far more fragile than it may appear to be. If Gould's vision of punctuated equilibrium is correct, then we could imagine that just before the outbreak of a mass extinction, the world might have seemed to have been more stable than it had appeared for a long time.

An economy, of course, is different from a natural system, especially since people associate stability with misfortune and even label stability as stagnation. People consider economic growth to be normal, and just before depressions, abnormal growth is taken to be the norm.

Admittedly, in making the case for punctuated equilibrium, I have been inconsistent in our use of the metaphor of natural selection. We have described natural selection as operating on individual firms, technologies, and maybe even industries. Metaphors, such as natural selection, only go so far and then they inevitably fall apart.

Most economists have a far more uncritical acceptance of the theory of natural selection than I do. Recall how Harvey Leibenstein infuriated George Stigler and, no doubt, many upholders of conventional economic dogma by indicating that natural selection in the form of competition might not be working its magic nearly as thoroughly as the textbooks would have us believe.

How would an economy appear prior to an outbreak of intense competition? The Leibenstein article implied considerable variation in performance between firms within the same industry during a period of lax competition, far more than would be consistent with an effective process of natural selection. My discussion of the social structure of accumulation implies that even though economic performance might vary a great deal, management forms might become relatively uniform.

The discussion of the evolution of product variety suggests that we might find little innovation of product form during such periods. Instead, we would expect to find products differentiating themselves through a proliferation of minor details rather than by virtue of some significant breakthrough in product design.

Of course, the presence of these symptoms does not prove that economic disaster is immanent. Nor will the absence of any of these elements ensure that the economy is absolutely free from danger.

CHAPTER 7

Managing Competition

Competitive Forces and Pricing in the Real World

Most economists now will readily accept that perfect competition does not actually exist in the real world. Some would argue, as the discussion of Harberger illustrates, that even though perfect competition may not exist, economic forces still compel firms to act as if something like perfect competition were at work. Other economists accept that some sectors of the economy are imperfectly competitive. In general, when these economists write of imperfect competition, they are directing our attention to an industry with a small number of firms, rather than to a characteristic of the economy as a whole. Within this context, a small number of firms might dominate an industry. Alternatively, brand loyalty might limit the degree to which consumers are willing to substitute one firm's product for another.

I would like to make two points about the imperfect competition literature: First, it treats the existence of imperfect competition as a characteristic of a specific industry. Second, it defines imperfect competition as the absence of perfect competition, as if perfect competition were the norm. In part, this approach has some merit. Certainly, the degree of competition does vary across industries. Some industries are obviously more competitive than others. A norm of perfect competition might be useful in the same sense that a norm of absolute zero temperature is: it provides a reference point even if we have never been able to discover it in the real world.

I am suggesting that we go considerably further. I propose that we take account of the fluctuations in the extent of competition over time. In other words, while the automobile industry is less competitive than agriculture, the competitive pressures that both industries feel will be stronger during a depression.

These fluctuating competitive pressures have very important ramifications for an economy. Suppose that the economy is in the midst of a severe depression. Firms that fear immanent bankruptcy will be desperate to keep a positive cash flow. They will go to great lengths to capture a larger market share from their competitors. Under such conditions, firms will be more than willing to drop prices toward marginal cost in the hopes that they can survive till prosperity returns, and then earn a profit.

Now assume that prosperity has returned. The surviving firms are less intent in jostling with their rivals. All firms would like to have more customers, but most may hesitate attempting to do so for fear of setting off a price war. Even if no such considerations are at work, as we will see below, light incentives do not seem to spur business to action. So as long as a business has plenty of customers, it does not display much interest in taking vigorous action to increase its market share.

Despite the textbook emphasis on competitive forces, strong competition is the exception rather than the rule. Gardiner Means noted that between 1929 and 1932, while the Great Depression was sweeping across the economy, motor vehicle prices fell only 12 percent, whereas production dropped by 74 percent. Other concentrated industries, such as agricultural implements, iron and steel, and cement demonstrated a pattern that was only slightly less extreme. Prices of agricultural commodities fell 54 percent, while output decreased by only 1 percent, but the oft-used example of agriculture was the exception rather than the rule (Means 1975: 10; citing National Resources Committee 1939: 386).

Most firms probably found themselves in conditions between those of the automakers and the farmers. In other words, even the Great Depression was not intense enough to force the economy as a whole to adopt marginal cost pricing. Nonetheless, textbook writers continue to insist on assuming marginal cost pricing, despite the enormous weight of contrary evidence (Lee 1984). In fact, when something approximating perfect competition appears in the real economy, we find adjectives other than *perfect* appended to the word competition. Rather than expressing appreciation of the benefits of perfect competition, we hear competition described as being excessive, ruthless, or cutthroat—a clear indication that those who witness conditions akin to perfect competition regard strong competition as unnatural—at least when it comes to be realized.

We still have to come back to an earlier question: Why do strong competitive pressures not make themselves felt the way the textbooks suggest that they should? I believe that we have to look at nonmarket forces for the reason that slight competitive pressure is the norm.

The Alleviation of Competition

Let us's take a moment to consider what might cause competition to break out within a seemingly stable social structure of accumulation. After a prolonged period of lax competition, profits begin to suffer, despite the absence of strong competition. Business begins to take on more and more staff. Lower-level workers begin to wrest some concessions from their employers. In effect, then, the measures used to protect the profit rate from competitive pressure eventually allow x-inefficiencies to eat away at profits.

As profits from productive activities sag, firms and investors will try to maintain their profit rate through speculative activity. While speculation might help to shore up profits for an individual investor or firm, speculation in itself does nothing to make an economy more productive. To make matters worse, speculation consumes considerable resources that could have otherwise been used for productive purposes. Admittedly, this tendency can work to the benefit of the profit rate, especially if speculators are consuming products that are subject to increasing returns—for example, computer software. Finally, speculative pressure takes a toll on the profits of productive firms to the extent that speculation bids up the prices of rents and raw materials.

At first, the negative effects of speculation may go unnoticed, because speculative profits can create an economic euphoria. Investors begin to overestimate the probable profit rates of their ventures as they become increasingly insensitive to risk. During such heady times, foolhardy investments will become commonplace. Finally, speculators will also inflate the stock and bond markets. The high price for financial assets will drag down the rate of profit in finance.

These conditions put the monetary authorities in a bind. If they continue to allow the speculative excesses to continue, the economy will become increasingly distorted. If they decide to bite the bullet and rein in speculation by tightening the money markets, competitive pressures will ratchet up. Prices, especially prices for stocks, bonds, and raw materials will become cheaper, while unemployment will soar. More often than not, this process, if left unchecked, will result in a severe recession or even a depression, especially if the speculation has been prolonged.

In the wake of the depression, the public will search out culprits: ghoulish monetary authorities, greedy speculators, or foolish management practices. In truth, all will play a role, but the stage was set by the prior lack of competitive pressures. A recession or depression will increase the level of competition.

Typically, the human costs of a depression are heavy. Even in the automobile industry, where prices fell relatively little during the Great Depression, employment fell sharply. Such are the demands of a market economy. Once the consequences of a competitive environment are felt by those who are accustomed to a more privileged position in the economy, the authorities shrink from allowing the competitive process to run its full course. Typically, they will step in with a looser monetary policy or expanded government spending—often on the military. With competition blunted again, the process will repeat itself.

Economists of a more libertarian persuasion will insist that the blame belongs with those who attempted to blunt the effect of competition in the first place. Alas, in the absence of these measures, an economic downturn would just as certainly occur, and perhaps with even more severity. Unfortunately, these downturns are far more savage than the libertarians acknowledge.

The Ambiguity of Competition

So far, I have followed the standard practice of economics in using the term *competition* in an admittedly loose manner. On the crudest level, industries are said to be either competitive or noncompetitive. For most economists, if competition is not rigorous enough, the fault must lie with government policies or collusion among corporations. In the absence of such interference with the market, strong competition will supposedly be the natural state of affairs. I agree with this conclusion, except that I maintain that under a regime of strong competition, crises will be the norm.

Specialists in industrial organization do have quantitative indices of the degree of competition. Typically, they look at the share of an industry held by the four largest firms. While this measure, known as a concentration ratio, appears to be objective or even scientific, many economists dismiss its relevance for several reasons.

In the first place, economists are hard pressed for an exact definition of an effective market. What is the market for a newspaper? Does my small-town newspaper compete against the *Wall Street Journal* or the *New York Times?* What about our free weekly newspaper? I could argue that the newspaper also competes with television, magazines, and even bowling, depending on how we understand the activity of reading a paper.

In addition, while many economists accept that high concentration ratios do exist, they dismiss any concern with that indicator. According to this school of thought, markets have merely determined the most effective outcome. High concentration ratios may be nothing more than evidence of the previous competitive success of the leading firms in the industry. The few remaining firms may just be so efficient that most of their rivals were too inefficient to survive. Lessening the powers of these successful companies would merely hobble the most efficient firms in the industry. Consequently, they argue that we should do nothing to tamper with the result.

Still others accept that the dominant firms might not necessarily have achieved their position as a result of prior efficiencies. Mergers or acquisitions might have eliminated some of the potentially most efficient firms. Even so, we should accept the high concentration because only the large firms are capable of mustering the forces required to achieve efficiency.

Although all parties in these debates differ in almost every other respect, we do find one constant theme: the presumption that the more competition, the better society will be. As Lester Telser, an exceptional economist who has taken the time to analyze the foundations of economic theory, wisely observed, "It is hard for many economists to accept the proposition that competition may be excessive because the received theory regards competition as always good, the more the better" (Telser 1987: 6–7).

To allow that too much competition can be destructive does not mean than competition serves no good purpose at all. In the absence of competitive pressures, few firms would be likely to exert themselves to strive for much efficiency—let alone maximum efficiency. Not many economists would disagree with the contention of John R. Hicks, a Nobel Prize winning economist, that in the absence of strong competitive pressures, those who run business will satisfy themselves with what Hicks called the "quiet life." In effect, with a relatively stable social structure of accumulation, business will mostly settle back and run on automatic pilot. Of course, business will, as always, look for profitable situations, but just not too hard.

At such times, the competitive system might have a few 400 hitters, but only because most of the competition is so lax. Mark Egnal tells two stories that illustrate the nature of lax competition. In 1956, Bethlehem Steel Corporation, the nation's second-largest steel producer, employed 11 of the 18 best-paid executives in the United States. Every vice president had his own dining room with linen tablecloths and full waiter service. Each Bethlehem plant had its own golf course, and the company employed three individuals whose only job was playing golf with clients (Egnal 1996: 163).

Egnal also reports that Pete Estes (who was soon to be appointed president of General Motors) turned thumbs down on a proposal in the early 1970s to introduce front-wheel-drive cars. He confided to a colleague: "When I was at Oldsmobile, there was something I learned that I've never forgotten. There was an old guy there who was an engineer, and he had been at GM a long time and he gave me some advice. He told me, whatever you do, don't let GM do it first" (Egnal 1996: 165; citing Halberstam 1986: 23). We may have some evidence of modest improvements under such conditions, but continuing with Gould's baseball metaphor, we will not see many home runs—at least in terms of major breakthroughs in productivity.

In sum, we have seen that firms require some sort of stress in order to prod them to be more efficient or even to pursue technical change energetically. Unfortunately, I cannot conceive of any rule that could apply in all or even most cases.

Egnal's two stories are a case in point. Pete Estes' reaction indicates a concern with a tradition, albeit a benighted tradition. Rewards of the nature of the perks of the Bethlehem executives should encourage long term planning and strategic thinking, since the flow of benefits would stop if the vice presidents underperformed or the company failed, as the Australian economist, John Legge, has reminded me. The present system of salaries and share options but no perks has removed the long-term incentive. .

In short, too much stress causes waste and great human losses; too little stress also causes waste and inefficiency. No economist, to my knowledge, has seriously addressed this question.

The closest I can come to a general proposition comes from an influential survey of the research on the state of industrial organization. The authors concluded that "a market structure intermediate between monopoly and perfect competition would promote the highest rate of inventive activity" (Kamien and Schwartz 1975: 32). So, we are left nothing more satisfying than an appeal to what I will later call "the Goldilocks principle."

Keeping Competition at Bay

While Martin Neil Baily was a member of President Clinton's Council of Economic Advisors he wrote: "Vigorous global competition against the best-practice companies not only spurs allocative efficiency, it can also force structural change in industries and encourage the adoption of more efficient product and process designs. . . . This conclusion represents a subtle departure from the standard view of competition" (Baily 1995: 308).

Baily's supposed "subtle departure" cries out for some explanation. If firms are always searching for the best business practices, why should the recent entry of foreign firms make this search significantly more effective? Baily seems to have stumbled onto a phenomenon that most economists have missed—that competitive pressures are variable.

Although business and government leaders eagerly pay lip service to their devotion to the principles of competition, in truth they go to great lengths to blunt competitive forces, relying on a number of tricks to keep competition at bay. Government regulations and tariffs protect domestic markets; government looks favorably on business cooperation and mergers; and finally, governments engage in stimulative monetary and fiscal policies. We normally do not consider expansionary monetary and fiscal policies to be anticompetitive, but additional buying power certainly does take some of the sting out of competition.

Even so, business, if economists' presumption about economic behavior were true, should still energetically seek out any means to increase profits. Such does not seem to be the case. Where competitive pressures are light, business does indeed seem to prefer the "quiet life" to the frenetic quest for maximum profits.

At the same time, as I mentioned before, economists are perfectly correct in believing that vigorous competition is the normal state of affairs, at least in the absence of measures, customs, or institutions that curtail competition. Where efforts to weaken competition are not present—whether collusion among firms, artificial stimulation of the economy, or protection through tariffs, quotas, or regulation—competitive forces will take on a momentum of their own. Prices will approach marginal costs, threatening to throw virtually all high fixed-cost producers into bankruptcy.

What Baily observed was the effect of a watershed moment when an economy, which was relatively protected from competition, suddenly began to feel the effect of competition from abroad—the unraveling of the regime of x-inefficiency that Harvey Leibenstein had discovered. One leading textbook on industrial organization had already pointed out evidence that strong import competition seems to blunt x-inefficiencies (Scherer and Ross 1990: 670). Of course, other factors were at work in influencing the economy, but I think that the delayed recognition of this shift marked the gulf between Baily's assertion and what he called "the standard view of competition."

Baily's description of the effect of the introduction of a heightened degree of foreign competition bringing an end to a period of the "quiet life" is comparable to an asteroid setting off a rapid evolutionary burst within the theory of punctuated equilibrium. The threat of imports from foreign producers forces domestic producers to embark on a series of defensive innovations in a belated effort to prevent imports (Wood 1995).

As we have mentioned before, economics departs from the story of punctuated equilibrium in one important respect: catastrophes in economics do not necessarily depend on some external event. Economic forces themselves generate catastrophes on their own. For example, if we think of the solar system as a whole, rather than life on earth, then events that might otherwise seem external, such as an asteroid crashing into earth, may be internal to the system.

The Goldilocks Principle of Competition

Now let us return to competition. Most economists cherish the idea that competition is unequivocally good, although some individuals may be hurt in the process. Keep in mind that competition is most intense during deep depressions. In fact, I am convinced that a depression is nothing else but an intensification of competition, whereas prosperity usually indicates a slackening of competitive pressures.

If more competition were always desirable, we should welcome depressions and rue their end. Of course, depressions are tragic events that take an immense toll on society. Yet some sort of oversight is necessary in any economy. In this sense, depressions do serve a useful purpose in a market economy, in the sense that they create pressures that coerce firms into finding new and better ways of doing business—including the creation of new social structures of accumulation.

Indeed, business responds to an outbreak of strong competitive pressures with a frantic search for efficiencies, but often apparently to no avail, at least in the short run. The absence of an immediate pay-off is to be expected for two reasons.

First, people often behave irrationally under stress. Indeed, many but certainly not all firms will make bad choices as they set off, under duress, to explore uncharted waters. Second, an even more important force is at work. Most of the firms and many of the workers are experiencing financial distress that causes markets to shrink at an alarming pace. For most firms, the rewards from successful innovations will have to wait until the return of a period of general prosperity.

A good many of the firms, even those firms that seem to be making the right decision in the midst of a depression, will not survive long enough to enjoy the fruits of their efforts. When competitive pressures become too intense, as they do during such times, they create mass economic extinctions, liquidating alike both efficient and inefficient firms, although an objective standard for determining which firms are efficient or inefficient at any moment is admittedly wanting.

At such times, survival of the fittest is certainly not operative. Like Gould's lungfish, a firm that may be tottering at the edge of extinction today might be ideally suited for the economic conditions that loom at the horizon. In any case, I have strong doubts that competitive forces are very selective once the full force of a depression is underway.

Only later, once the competitive pressures let up, will we see the benefits from the competitive struggle. Then, as the depression gives way to a stronger economy, the first fruits of the depression-era struggles will begin to appear. At that point, we will see business beginning to apply new technologies and to market new products. Such times resemble the flourishing periods following the mass extinctions that the paleontologists describe.

We might be tempted to think of an optimal level of competition, an intensity that would somehow neither force the economy into depression nor let business become too lax. In reality, the appropriate level of competition will vary according to economic conditions. Immediately following a depression, business enterprises will be taut—or, following the fashionable expression of recent times, lean and mean. Strong competitive pressures will serve little purpose at that moment. Later, as the recovery begins to age, an increasingly strong competitive pressure might become appropriate.

Such considerations never arise in mainstream economic literature. Few economists ever consider the possibility that competition can become too intense, although a handful of economists have recently developed theoretical models to indicate that excessive competition is likely to be the norm in an unregulated market (Stiglitz 1981; Suzumura and Kiyono 1987; Suzumura 1995; and Vickers 1995). This analysis has had virtually no impact on the thinking of economists in general.

Instead, most economists also assume that in the absence of collusion or protection by the government, competition can never become either too feeble or too strong. Like Goldilocks' porridge, the extent of competition will never be too hot or too cold.

Simulating Competitive Pressures

The notion of lax competition violates a central principle of economics. Economists presume that a market economy will naturally be competitive because business is supremely rational, so much so that no profitable opportunity could go unnoticed. In other words, even if expansionary monetary or fiscal policies were to relieve some competitive pressure, no company would rationally forgo a chance to earn some extra profit. As Adam Smith postulated long ago, "Every individual is continually exerting himself to find out the most advantageous employment for whatever capital he can command" (Smith 1776, IV.ii.4: 454).

Despite the confidence of Smith and his latter-day disciples, credible evidence for this belief is lacking; in fact, case after case suggests just the opposite to be true. Some of my favorite examples occur in response to environmental regulation. Invariably, industry howls at the very thought of environmental regulation. Once the regulations are imposed, business often finds that the regulation actually prodded business into saving money.

For example, in a recent study of major process changes at ten manufacturers of printed circuit boards, pollution control personnel initiated 13 of 33 major changes. Of these 13 changes, 12 resulted in cost reduction, 8 in quality improvements, and 5 in extension of production capabilities (Porter and van der Linde 1995a: 122; see also Porter and van der Linde 1995b; and Jaffe, Peterson, Portney, and Stavins 1995).

Similarly, Michael Porter and Claas van der Linde looked at the antipollution efforts at 29 chemical plants. Out of 181 waste-prevention activities, just one resulted in a cost increase. Most required little or no capital outlay. The average effect on product yield, where such information was available, was a 7 percent increase. For every dollar the plants spent complying with the waste-reduction regulations, they saved $3.49 (Porter and van der Linde, 1995a: 125). After reviewing a number of such cases, the authors concluded:

> The belief that companies will pick up on profitable opportunities without a regulatory push makes a false assumption about competitive reality—namely, that all profitable opportunities for innovation have already been discovered, that all managers have perfect information about them, and that organizational incentives are aligned with innovating. In fact, in the real world, managers often have highly incomplete information and limited time and attention. (Porter and van der Linde 1995a: 127)

The less-than-thorough effort to increase profit by controlling discharges of waste in the absence of regulation is not entirely surprising. These results are in line with some other evidence that suggests that business may be more inclined to vigorously reduce wages than to invest in other types of cost savings. Some business sources attribute this tendency to the ease in identifying wage costs compared to indirect costs, which cannot be pinpointed so precisely. Anne Carter's suggestion that "changes that economize direct labor are favored because they are more readily evaluated with today's information on wages and capital goods prices" does not seem particularly convincing (see Carter 1970: 218–9).

Alternatively, engineers are allegedly instructed to pursue single-mindedly the goal of developing methods to reduce labor inputs, without regard for the criterion of cost minimization. This practice is presumably designed to minimize the problems due to the perceived unreliability of labor (Piore 1968; see also Amsden and Brier 1977). This hypothesis finds modest support in Carter's analysis of the U. S. national input-output tables. The direct-labor coefficients decrease over time in almost all sectors, whereas no other pattern is discernible for other inputs (Carter 1970).

We should also take note of the effect that regulations will have on companies outside of the affected industry. The initial effect is likely to be an increase in the cost of pollution-control technologies. As firms vie to develop such technologies, the price of their products will fall. Turning to Adam Smith again, we find that more than two centuries ago he noted: "The increase of demand, beside though in the beginning it may sometimes raise the price of goods, never fails to lower it in the long run. It encourages production, and thereby increases the competition of the producers, who, in order to undersell one another, have recourse to new division of labour and new improvements of art, which might never otherwise have been thought of" (Smith 1776, V.i.e.26: 748).

Not only can we expect to see the price fall, but the effectiveness of such technology will also certainly improve.

Porter and van der Linde in effect reaffirm my contention that under normal competitive conditions, firms do not seek out all profitable opportunities, even in their own business. Although most economists rightly look to the government as a source of the weakening of competitive forces, they fail to acknowledge that government regulations can also simulate competitive pressure.

Slowly, a few leading corporate executives are coming to see the enormous profit potential arising from the simulated competition of environmental mandates, although the corporate sector initially resisted environmental mandates tooth and claw. For example, the chairman and CEO of 3M and the chairman of Dow Chemical have recently joined forces to write a book praising the economic potential of sustainable economic development, although they attribute progress in this arena to the foresight of business rather than to the outside pressures that forced business to recognize its own interests (Desimone and Popoff 1997).

Government can also stimulate competitive pressure through the vigorous enforcement of antitrust laws. Again, although firms violently protest government interference in such matters, such laws actually may serve business' best interests. One study compared the fates of U.S. firms that respectively won or lost antitrust cases in the early years of the Sherman Act. The authors found that the firms that succeeded in blocking the government's attempt to fragment their organization subsequently withered once international competition became more important, while those that lost their antitrust cases eventually prospered (Comanor and Scherer 1995).

Alice Amsden's analysis of Korea's successful industrialization drive suggests still another example of simulated competition. Korea's huge conglomerates, the *chaebol,* enjoyed a tremendous growth (Amsden 1989). Until Korea agreed to financial liberalization, the state controlled the financial system. The state was liberal in granting credit and subsidies, so long as the borrowing *chaebol* could substantially increase its exports in specified sectors. Should it falter, credit would be withheld. This demand created a powerful pressure to develop more competitive methods of production. This policy seemed to work quite well, at least until financial liberalization gave the *chaebol* easy access to credit without government conditions attached.

Inducing Technical Change

We can find hints of simulating competitive pressure in the early literature of political economy. A number of early writers observed that in the long run, apparent difficulties may actually promote growth. For example, a long tradition held that the Dutch became prosperous because of their lack of natural resources, which required that they be industrious (for example, see Hume 1752: 357). This idea became so widespread that "a Dutch fetish exercised its influence over English writers" (Furniss 1920: 101). Robert Houghton reflected the spirit of this British attitude, writing: "I will not wish such Necessity upon our selves in order to the like Improvements; but if for our Sins, through War, or any other Calamity, we shou'd be reduc'd . . . we may then say like David, 'Twill be good for us that we have been afflicted' (Houghton 1693–1703 (15 November 1695); cited in Baird 1997: 515).

The eighteenth-century tradition, however, mostly seemed to imply that the Dutch worked harder rather than smarter to compensate for their poverty of natural resources. I do not recall writers of the time indicating that the scarcity prodded the Dutch to pursue technical improvements, other than more careful farming techniques.

More recently, Albert O. Hirschman has popularized the idea of hardships being advantageous with his concept of "inducement mechanisms" (Hirschman 1958: 24–8). Hirschman did not emphasize natural deficiencies, such as the Dutch experienced, but the sort of disorder he found in Latin American economies of the time. He suggested that there might be an "optimum disorderliness" that is most conducive to economic growth (Hirschman 1971: 76).

Let us return to Michael Porter's position again. In an earlier work, he offered the sweeping proposition: "Disadvantages in basic factors are part of what jars firms away from resting on basic factor costs and into seeking higher-order advantages. In contrast, local abundance of basic factors lulls firms into complacency and deters the application of advanced technology. The resulting competitive advantages are often fleeting as is productivity growth" (Porter 1990: 83).

Porter then went on to say: "Factor disadvantages that stimulate innovation must be selective to motivate and not discourage, involving some but not all factors. Lack of pressure means there is rarely progress, but too much adversity leads to paralysis. . . . Too much pressure can lead to adaptive rather than to innovative investment behavior" (Porter 1990: 83).

An economy can simulate what we think of as natural competitive pressures in any number of ways. Nathan Rosenberg, perhaps the more preeminent economist on the subject of technology, has uncovered a number of examples to show how wars, strikes, and other difficulties have promoted the development of new technology (Rosenberg 1969). For example, consider the challenge that the oil crisis of the 1970s presented. For many decades, industry, especially in the United States, had predicated its industry on cheap oil supplies. Suddenly, it had to rethink its methods of production. Again, as was the case with environmental regulations, many firms rose to the occasion.

For example, prior to the energy crisis, supermarkets used to display frozen food in open freezers. In the face of higher prices, someone thought to put flexible plastic over the freezers to reduce energy costs. This almost obvious innovation probably reduced the cost of operating these freezers below what the expense of running them had been before energy costs rose.

Perhaps the greatest stimulus to such innovation comes from the pressure of rising wages. Today, with the process of globalization looming so large, policy makers have been intent on becoming competitive by keeping wages as low as possible—what I have elsewhere called "The Haitian Road to Development" (Perelman 1993, Ch. 1). Later, in my discussion of the history of competitive forces in the U. S. economy, I will elaborate on the constructive importance of this particular form of competitive pressure.

Simulating Competition and Manufacturing Crises

Simulated competition, just like what we normally think of as competition, need not necessarily serve a positive purpose. To illustrate this point, let us turn to the theories of Michael Jensen of Harvard University. According to Jensen, the highly paid managers who normally run large corporations have evolved into a collection of selfish bureaucrats who use corporate resources for their own aggrandizement. In effect, Jensen contends that normal competition is too weak to coerce managers to make their firms efficient (Jensen and Meckling 1976).

Even those managers who might forgo the perks of office do not necessarily act in the best interest of their shareholders. Instead, they typically concentrate on making the firm grow, whether or not that growth is economically warranted.

Isn't corporate growth an indication of managerial success? In terms of economic reasoning, the answer must be "not necessarily." Resources should go to those activities that are most productive. If a firm is not particularly productive, management might be well advised to direct the flow of resources away from that firm to another activity, rather than pursuing internal growth as an end in itself.

For example, suppose a firm is in an industry already burdened by excess capacity. With additional investment, the firm could grow by taking market share away from its competitors. Suppose further that, even if the firm were refurbished, it would be only marginally superior from the firms from which it captures market share. By withholding investment from this firm, management could free up resources to flow to those activities where they could earn the highest rate of return, which would exceed the highest possible profits from internal investment.

Instead, Jensen complained, managers of less productive firms aspire to maximize the amount of resources within the specific organizations that they control. As evidence of this perverse managerial behavior, Jensen cites the investigations of Gordon Donaldson, who studied 12 of the Fortune 500 corporations. In his study, Donaldson concluded that managers of these firms were not driven by maximization of the value of the firm but rather by the maximization of "corporate wealth," defined as the "aggregate purchasing power available to management for strategic purposes" (Jensen 1986: 323; citing Donaldson 1984: 3).

According to Donaldson, "In practical terms it is cash, credit, and other corporate purchasing power by which management commands goods and services" (Donaldson 1984: 27). In other words, management "satisfices" rather than optimizes.

Given management's penchant for feathering its own nest rather than promoting the health of the firm, Jensen concluded that "the problem is how to motivate managers to disgorge the cash rather than investing it at below the cost of capital or wasting it on organizational inefficiencies" (Jensen 1986: 323). Jensen contended that corporate takeovers are an ideal means to accomplish the goal of transferring cash out of the firm (Jensen and Ruback 1983).

In effect, he advocated corporate takeovers as a means of simulating competition. Stephen Nickell, an economist from Oxford University, and his co-workers came even closer to the notion of simulated competition. They proposed that financial market pressure and shareholder control might offer a substitute for product market competition. Using data from 580 manufacturing companies in the United Kingdom, they found that competition in product markets, as well as their variant of simulated competition, were associated with some degree of increased productivity growth (Nickell, Nicolitsas, and Dryden 1997).

The Dual Nature of Simulated Competition

Let us take a closer look at Jensen's vision of simulated competition. When one firm takes over another, the acquiring firm transfers significant funds to the shareholders of the acquired firm. Typically, the acquiring firm lacks sufficient funds to complete the purchase. As a result, it has to take on debt to complete the transaction.

Jensen welcomed this accumulation of corporate debt, believing it to be in the public interest. He argued that "the debt created in a hostile takeover (or takeover defense)" means "that it [the firm] cannot continue to exist in its old form" (Jensen 1988: 30). Once corporate managers no longer control great cash hoards, companies can no longer finance major capital expenditures from internal funds, unless the company has an enormous cash flow. Managers will have to turn to bankers or the capital markets to compete for funds. Jensen argues that bankers will only lend to highly profitable ventures. As a result, capital will flow more easily to those activities where it can be most productive. In fact, the management of these restructured companies will typically have to scramble to raise enough money just to pay off the interest on the accumulated debts. By creating a "crisis to motivate cuts," management must take measures that would otherwise be unthinkable (Jensen 1988: 30).

The mere threat of a takeover will also push firms in the same direction as an actual takeover. An enormous amount of cash makes a firm into a choice target for a takeover. Managers realize that in the wake of a takeover, the new owners will probably displace the existing management. Rather than leaving a tempting pool of cash on hand, firms make themselves a less desirable prey for a potential takeover by disgorging themselves of cash and taking on debt.

So far as Jensen is concerned, if the debt pushes the company near the brink of bankruptcy, so much the better. With the firm's very survival in question, managers must rise to the challenge to make the firm competitive. In addition, banks and other providers of corporate finance will monitor the firm more closely, knowing that the acquiring firm has to struggle to earn enough cash to cover its debt payments (Jensen 1986: 323).

Jensen often used the petroleum industry as a prime example of the potential benefits of restructuring (Jensen 1988: 33), but a closer examination of that industry raises some doubts about his theory. Consider the case of Exxon. Management restructured the company during the 1980s to make it a less attractive target for takeover specialists. The company engaged in severe cutbacks but not necessarily of the kind that make for a more efficient company.

According to a report in the *Wall Street Journal,* management forced Exxon's workers to become stretched too thin, but not in a manner that was conducive to efficiency. Several fires broke out in the company's largest refinery in Baytown, Texas, because Exxon was too tightfisted when it came to winterizing pipes against freezing, despite prior warnings about the danger (Sullivan 1990).

Many observers believe that this restructuring was ultimately responsible for Exxon's most famous mishap, the tragic oil spill of the *Exxon Valdez.* Alaskan officials allege that Exxon's systems for training and monitoring employees were ineffectual. The company's own tanker captains complained of heavy crew cutbacks and other unsafe operating procedures. Numerous former Exxon executives claim that management's cost cutting system "created an accident prone system" (Welles 1990: 75).

In fairness, we should note that some of Exxon's negligence predated its restructuring. Nonetheless, no one can doubt that corporate restructuring exacerbated the problems. What happened at Exxon may have been extreme, but we have no reason to believe that it was unique.

As Amitai Etzioni once observed, "A large body of research shows that under stress people's decision-making becomes less rational" (Etzioni 1988: 73). Most people can walk for 50 feet on a narrow plank that lies on the ground. Let that same plank span a ravine with a 1,000-foot drop and that same walk can become an exercise in stark terror. The fear of falling can make worry about falling become so intense that falling becomes a foregone conclusion. Corporate pressures can induce equally irrational responses.

Finally, we should note that the effect of high debt in the United States does not seem to have impelled firms to increase productivity by finding new and improved methods of organizing production. Instead, they seem to have preferred to cut back on wages by downgrading labor.

Indeed, the central thrust of the management system, which Jensen so lavishly praised, was to attack labor. In one famous study of the takeover of Transworld Airlines, Andrei Shleifer and Lawrence Summers estimated that the costs savings to the company was $200 million per year in wages just from pilots, mechanics, and flight attendants (Shleifer and Summers 1988). The value of this wage subsidy was far greater than what the takeover added to the company's worth, even when we take the stock market's excessively optimistic estimate of that value.

Taking Stock of Competition

Economists have never sorted out some important questions surrounding the nature of competition. To begin with, the biological metaphor cannot be pushed too far. Biological necessity may impel a Robinson Crusoe to bestir himself to procure food. The thirst for profit might even be the major incentive for corporate management. Nonetheless, in an economy increasingly dependent on individual creativity, we might question if the sole reliance on material rewards is the best way to inspire people. So, while competition might be a factor in the promotion of efficiency, at least we need to be open to alternative methods.

Even if an economy is organized around competition, we need to consider how that competition can sustain itself. Does an economy naturally tend to a system of monopolistic industries or will it have a large number of small but vital competitors?

I contend that the former is more likely because of the destructive nature of competition. I do not attribute this tendency toward destructive competition to the competitive nature of businesspeople. Instead, the structure of the industry compels them to act competitively. When an industry has increasing returns or a large fixed-cost industrial structure, only a few competitors could possibly survive. Moreover, strong competition will push prices to a level that will spell bankruptcy for all producers, unless measures are taken to limit competition.

The structure of an industry made up of a large number of small producers with relatively low fixed costs could possibly be stable. Nonetheless, the profit structure of these industries will not be healthy. Since such industries make up a small portion of the overall economy, large numbers of people seeking self-employment will probably flood these industries, ensuring that the profit rate will typically be depressed.

We have not seen this tendency toward destructive levels of competition occur very often in recent years. We could point to a handful of industries that have fallen under extreme price pressure, but not very many.

A number of factors have combined to limit the scope of competition. In the next chapter, I will discuss the reasons for the lack of competitive pressures in the United States since the Great Depression. I will also make the case that a number of long standing regulations, as well as institutions and conventions that predate market economies, work to limit competition. In the absence of these barriers to competition, our market economy would become unbearably unstable.

The Economy of High Wages

Jensen's method of simulating competition, like intense product market competition, has a tendency toward deflation. In Jensen's case, firms' responses add to the deflationary pressure. As they cut their wage bill, they diminish aggregate demand. Even though higher returns in the form of interest and profit may partially offset the lower wages, those who benefit from these sources of income tend to have a lower propensity to consume than workers do.

Let me suggest one form of simulated competition that does not pose the same risk as Jensen's form of simulated competition, namely, high wages. By keeping wages high, firms feel the same pressure to cut costs as they would by facing a high debt burden. High wages induce firms to concentrate on discovering capital-intensive methods to economize on labor. Such technologies represent the driving force of productivity growth.

For example, after the General Strike in Britain, the mining industry instituted wage cuts and the lengthening of working hours. Falling real wages, far from promoting investment, retarded the modernization of the industry. The legacy of this move towards a low-wage system was technological stagnation rather than prosperity (Fine, O'Donnell, and Prevezer 1985, 314–15).

Besides encouraging superior technology, high wages stimulate demand. To the extent that high wages protect the economy from falling into a recession or a depression, society will reap enormous benefits. Take the example of unemployment. We know that unemployment imposes steep costs on its victims. For each 1 percent increase in unemployment, we can expect to see 3,300 admissions to state prisons within six years. Other unemployed workers internalize their predicament, jeopardizing their health. For each 1 percent increase in unemployment, we can expect to see 37,000 deaths, 920 suicides, 650 homicides, 500 deaths from cirrhosis of the liver, and 4,000 admissions to state mental hospitals (Bluestone 1988: 34; and Bluestone and Harrison 1982: 63–66).

Moreover, society will be able to reap the benefits from the innovations in firms that would otherwise be swept away by the depression. Of course, we cannot even begin to calculate the full menu of human costs that depressions leave in their wake. I will return to this subject in the next chapter where I will discuss how high wages have promoted economic growth and development in the history of the United States economy.

The idea that high wages represent a healthy stimulant to the economy once was a commonplace idea among economists in the United States. This idea has fallen from view in recent years. I wish that I could say that I am mystified about why this once-popular idea is all but forgotten today. Were this idea fallacious, we would expect to see the refutation repeated in every textbook. Economists love to show how their "scientific method" can disprove popular conceptions. In fact, here is a theory that dates back to the dawn of economic theory. Moreover, this theory seems to confirm the central notion of supply and demand: namely, that a high price will induce agents to economize. Yet we hear nothing about the economy of high wages.

Instead, we hear the inverse over and over again; that a low price of labor will encourage employers to hire more workers. At best, we will hear an acknowledgment of the Keynesian caveat that low wages could possibly detract from aggregate demand. Alas, the idea that high wages will encourage productivity is virtually nowhere to be heard in mainstream economic literature.

I anticipate that those who are skeptical about the efficacy of a regime of high wages would be inclined to raise the objection that low wages are our first line of defense against the dread specter of inflation. Indeed, we find that business often attributes price increases to wage pressures.

I would like to suggest an alternative theory about the association of high wages and inflation: free from the lash of strong competition, firms use the cover of prosperity to gouge their markets rather than expending the effort to increase profits by new innovations. Despite the explanations by business, wage increases do not seem to cause inflation.

The relationship between wage growth and inflation does exist, but the causality runs in the reverse direction. Inflation seems to cause wages to rise rather than wage growth being responsible for setting off inflation (Mehra 1991; Gordon 1988).

I do not mean that wage increases never add to costs; however, in many industries, wage increases will ultimately lead to price decreases. Of course, in some cases, firms may not be able to recoup wage increases, but in others, the savings will more than pay for themselves (see the evidence in Levine 1992).

Of course, not all the benefits of high wages come from the wisdom and insight of managers. Highly paid workers who feel that they are treated fairly are more likely to apply their creativity to improving the production process. Conversely, workers who consider themselves to be unfairly exploited often act in ways to subvert the production process.

Serious consideration of the economy of high wages leads to the conclusion that economics can no longer treat labor as a passive force that must merely accept whatever the market offers. Instead, economists will have to recognize that labor's will plays a positive role in the economy. In an era of neoliberal absolutism, this idea does not sit very well.

Of course, high wages are not some sort of magic wand that can miraculously transform the economy. Many problems stand in the way. For example, capital flight can short circuit the possibility of an economy of high wages. Unfortunately, we may be entering an era in which footloose capital will leave national economies no choice but to compete by keeping wages low. Under this sort of regime, we can expect to see less intensive technical change, at least until the world's pool of low-wage economies is exhausted. In the interim, the downward pressure of high wages will mean that the standard of living for workers is likely to fall in the rich countries.

Even so, I do not think that the possibility of capital flight has anything to do with the economics profession's silence regarding the economy of high wages.

A Concluding Note on Fluctuating Competitive Pressure

I wholeheartedly agree with Michael Jensen that the mainstream of economics has missed the boat with respect to taking account of the variability of competition. Where competitive pressures are weak, management does become somewhat lax. For the past half century, such lax conditions have been the rule rather than the exception.

Jensen, like most economists today, maintains that competition is unequivocally good. While I do not deny that competition can enforce a certain degree of discipline on business, I have also noted that competition, both real and simulated, can be destructive. In this respect, I part company with Jensen.

At the same time, I have argued that simulated competition can promote economic welfare in ways that market-driven price competitive pressures do not. For example, market-driven price-competition can create a downward spiral culminating in a depression.

CHAPTER 8

A Thumbnail Sketch of the Evolution of Competition in the U.S. Economy

The Origins of the U.S. Economy

The United States of America stands today as the spearhead of the movement to turn the reins of society over to the market. This position is ironic in light of the history of that nation. What follows is a thumbnail sketch of the nature of competition in the history of the United States.

The United States emerged out of a collection of colonies that Britain regulated as tightly as it could, given the transportation and communications technologies of the day. Britain regarded the colonies as a means of strengthening the empire as a whole. Toward this end, the mother country determined what should not be manufactured in the colonies, where the colonial exports should go, and in whose ships.

The colonies fought a revolution against British mercantilism, but not against mercantilism. Instead, the Revolutionary War—at least in the eyes of those who wound up in control of the new nation—reflected a belief in the "need for utilizing the principle [of mercantilism] exclusively for colonial ends" (Hartz 1948: 6).

After the revolution, the leaders of the new republic were far more concerned with political rather than economic instability. They found themselves facing an unruly populace that took advantage of the new electoral democracy to challenge the power of business. The articles of confederation under which new the government operated was inadequate to check the popular pressure. In 1786, General Knox, whose name was appropriately immortalized in the nation's famous fort of gold, captured the spirit of the times in complaining to George Washington about small farmers:

"Their creed is 'That the property of the United States has been protected from the confiscations of Britain by the joint exertions of all, and therefore ought to be the common property of all.' . . . In a word, they are determined to annihilate all debts, public and private, and have agrarian laws, which are easily effected by means of unfunded paper money which shall be a tender in all cases whatever" (Hacker 1940: 185).

To meet the popular threat, a small group within the congress of the new government won approval to make a few technical changes to the existing system of government. It invited every state to send delegates in May 1787 "for the sole and express purpose of revising the Articles of Confederation adequate to the exigencies of government and the preservation of the Union" (Bourgin 1989: 12).

From the beginning, this group intended to exceed its mandate. These people took it upon themselves to frame an entirely different governmental structure. They did so as far from the public eye as possible. From the first day, the Constitutional Convention was sworn to secrecy. Even though it was a hot summer, they closed the windows to prevent eavesdropping (Bourgin 1989: 12–13).

A number of irregularities marred the ratification process. For example, even before the Framers presented the Constitution to the Congress, they were trying to get the Pennsylvania legislature to set up a ratifying convention. Nineteen assemblymen who supported the radical Pennsylvania Constitution of 1776 decided to block ratification by staying away from the legislature to prevent a quorum. A Federalist mob went to the homes of two of the more radical assemblymen and dragged them through the streets to the assembly in order to create a quorum. The process was so rushed that a good number of voters did not even know about the election. Of the 70,000 eligible voters, only 13,000 voted in the election (Fresia 1988: 64).

In Massachusetts, opponents to the Constitution had the majority. Rather than accept defeat, proponents agreed to a plan to ask for amendments to the Constitution. The Federalists proposed a number of popular amendments. Based on this representation, ratification succeeded, although the amendments were never considered. Virginia Federalists followed a similar strategy (Boursin 1989: 64).

In New Hampshire, the majority of the delegates were elected on the basis of opposing ratification, but a number of them did not vote the way that their electorate instructed them to. In New York, two thirds of the delegates were opposed to the Constitution, but the promise to work for a new convention swayed enough of them to vote for ratification. Rhode Island and North Carolina rejected ratification outright (Boursin 1989: 65).

While the opponents of the new constitution tended to be those with the least connection to markets, the new government was not at all dedicated to laissez-faire. Among the government's central policy initiatives were a protectionist tariff and bounties to select producers. The tariff was all the more effective because foreign competitors also had to overcome the cost of transporting goods from the Old World to the New.

One other factor limited competition: the corporation—but not the great multinational organizations that we see today. Indeed, the modern corporate form was still unknown at the time. Instead, according to one study: "The corporation was conceived as an agency of government, endowed with public attributes, exclusive privileges, and political power, and designed to serve a special function for the states. Turnpikes, not trade, banks, not speculations, were its province because the community, not the enterprising capitalists, marked out this sphere of activity" (Handlin and Handlin 1945: 22).

Within this context, the government only granted corporate status to a few select businesses, whose operations appeared to serve a public interest, such as the provision of bridges or roads or banking. Despite the high-minded public purpose of the corporation, those who won corporate charters often did not act in the public interest. Instead, they were generally people who took advantage of their close ties to government officials.

Jacksonian Neoliberalism

The first brush with a more thoroughgoing market control came during the presidency of Andrew Jackson. The rising entrepreneurial class, which lacked the political connections to profit from the lucrative corporation charters, represented one of the largest constituencies behind the Jacksonian movement.

One writer astutely characterized the Jacksonian period as "the democracy of expectant capitalists" (Simons 1925: 210). Another offered the following description of the leaders of the Jacksonian movement: "People were led as they had not been before by visions of money-making. Liberty became transformed into laissez faire. A violent, aggressive, economic individualism became established. . . . It opened economic advantages to those who had not previously had them; yet it allowed wealth to be concentrated in new hands only somewhat more numerous than before, less responsible, and less disciplined" (Hammond 1957: 327).

The leaders of the Jacksonian era abolished the Bank of the United States to allow for an unregulated banking system. They severely limited the federal provision of infrastructure, although the states continued to be actively involved. Nonetheless, the Jacksonians were not dogmatic advocates of laissez-faire. Many of them just wanted to get rich. In this spirit, they attacked whatever inconvenienced them in this endeavor. As a result, the erection of higher tariff barriers to protect the emerging industrial structure did not necessarily offend their principles. Nor did the brutal relocation of Native Americans or the extension of slavery seem to trouble them unduly.

As is often the case, a severe depression ended this get-rich-quick episode. Peter Temin insists, with good cause, that neither the destruction of the Bank of the United States nor the subsequent speculation caused the depression (Temin 1969). According to Temin, the Bank of England's efforts to tighten monetary conditions in Britain caused the depression. I see no reason to question his analysis. No one, to my knowledge, has ever uncovered a serious flaw in his book on the Jacksonian period. This immunity from criticism makes Temin's book unique in modern economics, a discipline, as we have already noted, known to challenge and dispute just about anything.

Even so, I suspect that Temin might have been overlooking a different sort of cause. During the Jacksonian period, the United States experienced a canal boom of enormous proportions. Temin reported that capital imports amounted to 5 percent of the gross national product in 1836 (Temin 1969: 84). This opening of the economy made continued prosperity dependent on a continuing inflow of capital, which the Bank of England effectively discouraged, with the tightening of monetary conditions. In this sense, the Jacksonians, by making the economy more vulnerable to international monetary conditions, did bear a responsibility for the depression.

I do not mean that in the absence of the Jacksonian revolution no depressions would have occurred. Indeed, lingering resentment of an earlier depression generally attributed to bank mismanagement helped the Jacksonians win in the first place. But I do believe that the Jacksonian push in the direction of laissez-faire made the depression deeper and more long lasting than it would have otherwise been.

The Rise of Republican Economic Control

In the wake of the Jacksonian depression came the formation and eventual triumph of the Republican Party. Most Americans identify the Republican Party with a challenge to slavery, but initially the party only proposed to limit the extension of slavery, not abolish it. Economic factors played a stronger role in the Republican vision for the United States.

First and foremost, the Republicans wanted to build up the domestic economy to take advantage of potential economies of scale. For example: "The initial investment for furnaces that used coal to heat iron ore was about 50 percent higher than required for charcoal furnaces; but the capacity of the anthracite furnaces was about double sometimes triple, that of comparable charcoal plants" (Livingston 1994: 29).

After the Jacksonians left office, the tariff had become weaker. For the Republicans, the tariff was a key to economic development. According to James Livingston: "The protective tariff in the platform . . . of 1860 was the critical device through which the resources hitherto consumed by the managers and beneficiaries of an Atlantic economy would be diverted to and invested in a home market" (Livingston 1994: 33–34). The Republicans believed that they could also encourage domestic industry by restricting immigration, which could (modestly) raise wages, thereby building domestic demand. The Homestead Act was an even more effective means of expanding domestic demand. Mechanization of prairie farming had already begun between 1846 and 1857. The Republicans calculated that the domestic capital goods industry could not prosper without an expansion of prairie farming or without some federal policy assistance (Livingston 1994: 24–25).

The Republicans never got the chance to test the efficacy of their measures to promote domestic industry. Instead, the Civil War created an even more extensive, planned economy. Industry expanded as never before. Out of this expansion came new technologies and the seed of what was to become an industrial supremacy.

The Economy of High Wages Again

How, with the restrictions on competitive behavior, did the United States manage to become such an efficient producer? Of course, high tariffs and high transport costs did not prevent foreign competition altogether. However, a much more important factor was at work.

The economy of the United States enjoyed a scarcity of labor, which forced manufacturers to search for labor-saving technologies. The labor-saving technologies, in turn, created a relative prosperity that allowed workers to demand still higher wages, inducing another round of technical change.

We are taught to fear high wages, but the historical record of the U. S. economy suggests that business did often manage to create new technologies fast enough to make prices fall, even in the face of rising wages.

Certainly, the rapidity of technical change struck most observers of the early United States. For example, the renowned French visitor, Alexis de Tocqueville, reported: "I accost an American sailor, and I inquire why the ships of his country are built so as to last for a short time; he answers without hesitation that the art of navigation is every day making such a rapid progress that the finest vessel would become almost useless if it lasted beyond a certain number of years" (de Tocqueville 1848, II: 420).

H. J. Habakkuk wrote an entire book about the positive effect of high wages on technical change in the United States during the nineteenth century. According to Habakkuk, "The Secretary of the Treasury reported in 1832, that the garrets and outhouses of most textile mills were crowded with discarded machinery. One Rhode Island mill built in 1813 had by 1827 scrapped and replaced every original machine" (Habakkuk 1962: 57; and the numerous references he cites).

The anticipation of early retirement of plant and equipment in the United States was so pervasive that manufacturers in the United States built their machinery from wood rather than more durable materials, such as iron (Strassman 1959: 88).

Throughout the nineteenth century, commentators continued to echo De Tocqueville's observation that technology in the United States was designed to be short-lived (Schoenhof 1893). For example, in the late nineteenth century, the U. S. Secretary of State commissioned Joseph Schoenhof to inquire into the effects of high wages on the competitiveness of business in the United States. Schoenhof concluded:

> The employer of labor is . . . benefited by the inevitable results of a high rate of wages. . . . [T]he first object of the employer is to economize its employment.
>
> Manufacturers introducing a change in manufactures have a machine built to accomplish what in other countries would be left to hand labor to bring about. Machinery, used to the limit of its life in Europe, is cast aside in America if only partially worn. (Schoenhof 1893: 33–34)

The Cornell economist, Jeremiah Jenks asserted: "No sooner has the capitalist fairly adopted one improved machine, than it must be thrown away for a still later and better invention, which must be purchased at a dear cost, if the manufacturer would not see himself eclipsed by his rival" (Jenks 1890: 254; cited in Livingston 1986: 39).

This pattern of rapid capital renewal made the manufacturing capacity in United States the envy of the world. By the turn of the century, exports from the United States were inundating Europe, much the same as Japanese exports displaced U.S. production in recent years. Just as people in the United States tried to discover the secret of Japanese ascendancy in popular books, English readers pored over alarmist books with titles, such as *The American Invaders* (1901), *The Americanization of the World* (1901), or *The American Invasion* (1902) (Wright 1990: 652).

By the late nineteenth century, rapid technical change had brought productivity in the United States to such a high level that the rationale for high wages seemed self-evident to most observers.

An Interruption in the Economy of High Wages

By the late nineteenth century, the downward pressure of competition began to overwhelm the upward thrust of high wages. Two factors help to explain this turn of events. First, the new technology of the post–Civil War period was very capital intensive compared to what had preceded it.

For example, in 1832, an entrepreneur could start a woolen mill with just over $1,000 (Kroos and Gilbert 1972: 106)—about the cost of beginning a homestead a few decades later (see Danhof 1941). Even in the iron industry, relatively simple technology sufficed before the Civil War. For example, Thaddeus Stevens, the famous radical Republican politician, wrote a letter to a military friend on 11 July 1863 informing him about the damage that the Confederate troops imposed on his iron mill: "They then seized my bacon (about 4,000 lbs.), molasses and other contents of the store—took about $100 worth of corn in the mills, and a like quantity of other grain. On Friday, they burned the furnace, saw-mill, two forges, and rolling mill" (cited in Hacker 1940: 259).

Louis Hacker, a prominent historian of the time, commented on this letter: "Stevens, in conjunction with a group of farms, ran a sawmill and iron works. His workmen, in addition to being employed in the works, undoubtedly must have labored on the farms, for the eighty tons of hay destroyed (according to the letter) was a sizeable quantity" (Hacker 1940: 259).

What did the bacon and molasses have to do with the manufacture of iron? They were used in his store to barter with his workers for their labor. As Hacker noted: "Thaddeus Stevens, as an iron master, had closer links with the cottage-and-mill system of production of sixteenth- and seventeenth-century England than with the industrial Pittsburgh of the 1870s" (Hacker 1940: 259).

Of course, some isolated examples of large-scale industry did exist prior to the Civil War. For example, in 1839, the Great Western Iron Company invested $500,000 in western Pennsylvania. By 1845, the Brady's Bend Iron Company in western Pennsylvania purchased the property. Among its holdings were:

> nearly 6,000 acres of mineral land and 5 miles of river front upon the Allegheny. It mined its own coal, ore, limestone, fire-clay, and fire-stone, made its own coke, and owned 14 miles of railway to serve its works. The plant itself consisted of 4 blast furnaces, a foundry, and rolling mills. It was equipped to perform all the processes, from getting raw materials out of the ground to delivering finished rails and metal shapes to consumers, and could produce annually between 10,000 and 15,000 tons of rails. It housed in its own tenements 538 laboring families. This company, with an actual investment of $1,000,000, was among the largest in America before the Civil War, though there were rival works of approximately equal capacity and similar organization. (Clark 1929: 446)

Even in the case of the Great Western Iron Company, the manufacturing operation does not sound terribly capital intensive, representing less than $2,000 per family. In all likelihood, this figure is too high, since many of the families would have had multiple workers. Nonetheless, few enterprises matched the scale of the Great Western operation. As Jeremy Atack correctly observed in his study of the changing industrial structure of the time, "The majority of manufacturing plants in most industries, even as late as 1870, operated on a modest scale" (Atack 1986: 462).

The impact of the subsequent modernization of industry in the United States was nothing short of amazing. The Bessemer process reduced the price of steel rails by 88 percent from the early 1870s to the late 1880s. During the same period, electrolytic refining reduced aluminum prices by 96 percent, and synthetic blue dye production costs fell by 95 percent (Jensen 1993: 835).

These price declines did not merely reflect technological progress. Because the new technology typically required a substantial increase in scale, the productive capacity for industrial products began to outstrip demand, putting downward pressure on prices.

In effect, the modern industrial structure, brought on in large part by the high wage pattern in the United States, was so effective that the pressure for high wages subsided. Again, other factors were involved. The new technologies allowed relatively unskilled workers to replace many of their more skilled counterparts. As a result, industrial employers could take advantage of the rapid flow of immigrants to the United States.

The Great Depression of the Late Nineteenth Century

The consequences of this downward pressure on prices were severe and long-lasting. One writer of the 1890s reported that the long depression, dating from 1873, was "unparalleled in the history of the world. It has been continuous during all these 20 years, though temporary and local causes have here and there tended to obscure the fact of continuity" (Cooke 1893: 597).

In the words of Joseph Schumpeter, writing during the Great Depression of the 1920s: "As far as mere figures go . . . some aspects . . . of the depression were quite as dark in 1873 to 1877 as they were in 1929 to 1933. . . . [I]f we . . . believe in the figure of 3 millions of 'tramps' (in the winter of 1873 to 1874) then this . . . would indicate that relative unemployment was actually worse than it was during the recent world crisis" (Schumpeter 1934, i: 337).

The wholesale price index fell from 135 in 1870 to 100 in 1880 to 82 in 1890. The prices of raw materials fell even faster (Mayhew 1990: 390). To make matters worse, the globalization of trade in grains was creating unheard-of levels of instability in agriculture, still the largest sector of the economy. In the words of Douglass North, a Nobel Prize-winning economist: "[The farmer in the United States] found himself competing in a world market in which fluctuations in prices created great uncertainty. The bottom might drop out of his income because of a bumper crop at the other side of the world—in Argentina or Australia" (North 1966: 134).

The wholesale price index fell from 135 in 1870 to 100 in 1880 to 82 in 1890. The prices of some of the homogeneous products fell even faster (Mayhew 1990: 390).

The depression did not make sense within the context of ordinary economic thought. Modern technologies were making great advances. Production was increasing, yet farmers and workers were suffering. More surprising, despite vigorous economic growth, profits were falling. People thrashed about to find explanations. In 1886, a Dutch committee ascribed the depression to "the low price of German vinegar"; and in Germany, some blamed it on the "immigration of Polish Jews" (Wells 1889: 21).

To their credit, many economists did realize what was happening: competitive forces were being unleashed. Unless something was done to hold competition in check, the economy would continue on a downward spiral. They argued for a system of trusts, cartels, and monopolies to limit competitive forces (Perelman 1996).

Ironically, at the same time that these economists recommended measures to keep competition in check, they published academic works proclaiming that perfect competition would lead to the best of all possible worlds (Perelman 1996). While the economy was still in the midst of the economic crisis, the notion of an equilibrium must have seemed less and less likely. Nonetheless, academic economists, such as Alfred Marshall in his influential *Principles of Economics* (1890), led a movement that "turned economics away from a concern about individual liberty toward an idea of market equilibrium" (Peritz 1996: 33).

Eventually, the crisis passed, but even laissez-faire economists attributed the end to external forces. For example, Milton Friedman credited the end of the deflationary policy to the gold discoveries of the 1890s (Friedman and Schwartz 1963: 135–7).

I am convinced that other far more important factors were at work in pulling out of the crisis. Deflationary pressures set off the great merger movements of the late nineteenth and early twentieth centuries. The great corporations that emerged from this process were strong enough to increase their profit margins. In addition, the government began a capital-intensive arms build-up together with a push to expand exports (see Perelman 1996).

Other governments followed suit in the scramble to expand exports. The resulting rivalry eventually culminated in the First World War. After postwar prosperity commenced, the United States confidently affirmed the rules of laissez-faire once again during the 1920s, setting the stage for another bout of competition, more popularly known as the Great Depression of the 1930s.

The Golden Age

The massive military demand from the Second World War pulled the economy out of the Great Depression. Although the U. S. government was quick to discard the benefits of wartime planning, it carefully crafted a military-industrial complex of lavish proportions. This system succeeded in curbing the destructive forces of competition by applying additional demand whenever the economy began to falter (Sherman 1983: 382).

Unfortunately, the Golden Age lost its luster after a few decades. Business, freed from the prod of competition, became increasingly inefficient. X-inefficiencies accumulated. Eventually, foreign competition became ever more severe. In recent years, business has avoided a repeat of the depression of the late nineteenth century. Profits have not collapsed, despite the seemingly increasing intensity of competition.

Why has business fared better at the end of the twentieth century than it did at the end of the nineteenth? First, business is enjoying an increasing advantage vis-à-vis labor. Unions are reeling. Business has outsourced even skilled labor to low-wage regions abroad. In effect, business has been able to transfer the competitive pressures onto labor, at least so far. The environment has absorbed additional pressure, as lax economic policies spared business the expense of environmental protection.

Perhaps the most important factor at business' disposal is the enforcement of intellectual property rights, which give certain kinds of firms protection from direct competition. Indeed, vigorous pursuit of the protection of intellectual property seems to be the highest international priority of the U. S. government.

CHAPTER 9

Inertia

Markets and the Benefits of Inertia

Let us now return to a recurrent question in this book: If markets have a tendency toward instability, why don't we see more evidence of this instability? A number of writers have come to the conclusion that markets do not display their full tendency toward instability because of other forces that manage to hold markets partially in check. For example, Piero Ferri and Hyman Minsky have noted: "In a world where the internal dynamics imply instability, a semblance of stability can be achieved or sustained by introducing conventions, constraints and interventions into the environment" (Ferri and Minsky 1991: 20; cited in Papadimitriou and Wray 1997: 494).

In some cases, organizations intentionally attempt to erect such constraints. For example, when the stock market begins to move too fast, so-called circuit breakers kick in to stop the market temporarily. These circuit breakers are intended to keep the market from spinning out of control.

Other constraints developed without any thought of contributing to the overall stability of the market. Whether their effect was intended or not, those forces that limit the movements of markets can still serve a vital purpose. In this respect, I think back to Schumpeter's earlier-cited assertion: "[R]estrictions . . . are . . . often unavoidable incidents, of a long run process of expansion which they protect rather than impede. There is no more of a paradox in this than there is in saying that motorcars are traveling faster than they otherwise would because they are provided with brakes" (Schumpeter 1950: 88).

Perhaps the most obvious example of a useful restriction on the economy comes from the work of John Maynard Keynes. Prior to Keynes, economists treated labor as if it were no different from any other commodity offered for sale on the market. If workers supplied too much labor, wages would fall until the supply of and demand for labor would be equated. Consequently, labor markets would always move toward an equilibrium without some sort of constraint. Conservative economists even suggested that the depth of the Great Depression was due to the ability of workers' organizations to prevent wages from falling to an equilibrium level.

Keynes, however, charged that "classical theory has been accustomed to rest the supposedly self-adjusting character of the economic system on the assumed fluidity [flexibility] of money-wages; and when there is rigidity, to lay on this rigidity the whole blame of maladjustment" (Keynes 1936: 257).

He then went on to add:

> To suppose that a flexible wage policy is a right and proper adjunct of a system which on the whole is one of laissez-faire, is the opposite of the truth. . . .
>
> [I]f labour were to respond to conditions of gradually diminishing employment by offering its services at a gradually diminishing money-wage, this would not, as a rule, have the effect of reducing real wages, and might even have the effect of increasing them, through its adverse influence on the volume of output. The chief result of this policy would be to cause a great instability of prices, so violent perhaps as to make business calculations futile in an economic society functioning after the manner of that in which we live. (Keynes 1936: 269)

In other words, since wages represent a large but shrinking part of the overall price system and wages tend to be "sticky," prices do not move nearly as quickly as they otherwise would have. In moderation, some wage flexibility might help to keep the economy in a rough balance, but too much wage flexibility would preclude a rational economy.

Just imagine what the world would be like if wages immediately responded to minute changes in the economic environment. Wages, especially in Keynes' day, represented a good portion of the cost of a typical commodity. If wages were unstable, prices would also be. Accordingly, stability in wages creates an inertia in prices, which facilitates calculations about the future. In the absence of such inertia, the economy could spin out of control. In effect, unchecked market forces could create the sort of price instability that economists often attribute to a severe inflation.

Keynes on Price Stability

Keynes believed that sticky wages provided a stability by serving as an anchor for prices. In this way, sticky wages maintain a degree of coherence most of the time. In an economy without the benefit of the inertia that sticky wages create, business could not budget for the future with any confidence. Yet confidence is essential to a dynamic economy.

For example, how could contractors feel comfortable bidding on the construction of an office building when they have no idea what the future prices of lumber, cement, or glass might be when the time comes to purchase them? A mistake can possibly throw them into bankruptcy. Some, of course, might recklessly hazard a bid. Others might do so rationally, but they would have to increase their expected profit margins substantially to compensate for the potential risk of failure. These higher margins will inhibit investment in factories and other investments built under similar bids.

In addition, unless prices and wages fall at roughly the same rate, great imbalances can occur. For example, if wages fall faster than prices, insufficient buying power can threaten an economic collapse. So wage stability, rather than causing problems, actually protects the economy against disaster. For example, in the case of the Great Depression, large employers in the United States tended to keep wage rates relatively steady until 1931. The upsurge in wage flexibility after that time coincided with the steepest phase of the economic decline (Perelman 1996: 139).

We should not be surprised that this part of Keynes' analysis never took hold, even though virtually an entire generation of economists declared themselves to be Keynesians. After all, to believe that price flexibility could be destabilizing threatened to undermine the core of mainstream economic theory.

With regard to wage and price flexibility, prior to the Great Depression, economists believed as a matter of course that depressions could dissolve through the magic of price flexibility. For example, in the midst of the Great Depression, Lionel Robbins, perhaps the most distinguished British defender of laissez-faire at the time, proclaimed: "a greater flexibility of wage rates would considerably reduce unemployment. . . . If it had not been for the prevalence of the view that wage rates must at all costs be maintained in order to maintain the purchasing power of the consumer, the violence of the present depression and the magnitude of the unemployment which has accompanied it would have been considerably less" (Robbins 1935: 186).

Robbins' view would have had some merit in the early nineteenth century, when small producers with little fixed capital predominated. By the time of the Great Depression, most branches of the industrial sector were sufficiently concentrated so that the effect of competition was muted. When demand evaporated in a concentrated industry, quantities rather than prices fell.

Recall Gardiner Means' observation that while prices plummeted in agriculture and very competitive sectors, in concentrated industries, prices were virtually unchanged. Similarly, Ellis Hawley concluded:

> A high degree of concentration, coupled typically with price leadership, oligopolistic understanding, cartel agreements, interlocking relationships, or the control of key patents, had largely eliminated price competition in such important and widely varying industries as automobiles, chemicals, motion pictures, farm implements, aluminum, cigarettes, newsprint, anthracite coal, glass containers, optics, lead, sulphur, and tin plate. . . . The FTC uncovered a wide variety of price-fixing, market-sharing, exclusive dealing, and production-restricting arrangements in such industries as plate glass, building supplies, caps, paper containers, print cloth, and petroleum refining. And such NRA innovations as the garment label, the automobile dealers' "Guide Book," and the copper cartel persisted long after the Blue Eagle was dead. (Hawley 1966: 166)

So, events disproved Robbins' theory. To his credit, Robbins eventually recognized that his undue faith in price flexibility was unwarranted.

Anticompetitive Forces and Stability

As a general rule, we might follow Keynes in recognizing that a degree of rigidity is probably helpful in preventing large shocks from destabilizing the economy. For example, I already mentioned that the attempt to hold wages steady in the United States during the early years of the Great Depression helped to maintain a degree of stability in the early months after the stock market crash.

Other forms of rigidity help to steady the economy. For example, as Keynes observed, since monopolistic firms face less uncertainty than a competitive firm, industrial concentration will tend to stabilize investment (Keynes 1936: 163). John Kenneth Galbraith made this same point even more forcefully: "Price stability also serves the purposes of industrial planning. Prices being fixed, they are predictable over a substantial period of time. And since one firm's prices are another's costs so costs are also predictable. Thus on the one hand prices facilitate control and minimize the risk of a price collapse that could jeopardize earnings and the autonomy of the technostructure" (Galbraith 1967: 194).

Schumpeter also made a similar case for restraining laissez-faire. Recall his earlier-cited assertion that "restrictions . . . are . . . often unavoidable incidents, of a long run process of expansion which they protect rather than impede. There is no more of a paradox in this than there is in saying that motorcars are traveling faster than they otherwise would because they are provided with brakes." (Schumpeter 1950: 88)

Schumpeter added: "inasmuch as we may assume that the refusal to lower prices strengthens the position of the industries which adopt that policy either by increasing their revenue or simply by avoiding chaos in their markets—that is to say, so far as this policy is something more than a mistake on their part—it may make fortresses out of what otherwise might be centers of devastation" (Schumpeter 1950: 95).

We should also take note that this same sort of inertia that Keynes, Galbraith, and Schumpeter advocated can prove to be dangerous when maintained too long, as they themselves recognized. For example, after World War II, many large firms in the United States used a combination of market power and protectionism to permit them to maintain their outdated plant and equipment, while Europe and Japan were deploying more modern technologies. This strategy allowed them to enjoy a greater degree of stability, at least in the short run, but it eventually left these same firms vulnerable to a competitive shock from imports during the 1970s and 1980s.

Prices, Information, and Ideology

In contrast to Keynes, laissez-faire conservatives tend to argue that flexibility presents no danger whatsoever. On the contrary, they maintain that flexibility is what makes markets so efficient. In effect, the conservatives accept on faith that the market would necessarily never be far from a state of equilibrium. In this way, they rule out the possibility of the sort of instability that troubled Keynes.

Each side in this debate is far better in finding the weakness of the opponent's case than in their own. Charles Kindleberger, one of the few people to approach the subject of the comparative performance of concentrated versus fragmented industries in an undogmatic fashion, in the end confessed agnosticism: "It seems to me worth historical exploration to ascertain whether the disability of a highly articulated system of small, independent firms, linked through a complex system of merchants and markets, is, for all its efficiency in production in a given state of the arts, less effective in responding to innovation elsewhere than vertically integrated firms" (Kindleberger 1961: 297).

In the end, historical research will never settle this matter. To begin with, the answer will probably vary according to the product life cycle and the relative importance of investment in long-lived capital goods within any industry. In addition, the difference between Keynes and conservatives reflects a deeper methodological gap. For the conservatives, the sort of impediments to stability that Keynes and Galbraith wanted to overcome was irrelevant. The conservatives see the world as being made up of large number of separate parts, which connect to each other only by way of transparent market relationships.

Given that they do not make allowance for strategic interdependence between various agents in their theory, the conservatives have no reason to believe that business decisions would be very complicated. In particular, firms will have no difficulty investing optimally in a laissez-faire environment. This conclusion emerges, in part, because according to the conservatives, prices will communicate all relevant information to anybody who knows how to read the market. Moreover, nobody could possibly improve on an outcome that results from profit-seeking agents responding to market signals.

For Keynes, in contrast, prices reflect only a small part of the total amount of information that would be needed to make correct decisions. After all, an investment is a decision that spills over into the unknowable future. Whether a decision turns out to be correct or not depends, at least in part, on the future actions of others. Prices could not conceivably be expected to convey accurate information about the future. Instead, investment occurs within a climate of pervasive uncertainty.

Keynes insisted that people's behavior can affect the outcome of others' actions either positively or negatively. For this reason, he saw the world as a strategic arena in which an individual is forced to make decisions in light of what she or he imagines the other person's future decisions to be.

Within this context, the economy can find itself swept up in information cascades where each person's actions reinforce other people's mistaken beliefs (see Anderson and Holt 1997). This process sometimes culminates in a crescendo of disaster. Inertia plays an important role in slowing down the pace of change, especially when speculation clouded ignorance drives events. Although decision makers still have to aim at moving targets, the speed within which these changes occur is slower. By creating an environment of semi-stability, people will be more willing to risk committing resources to an uncertain future.

I suspect that Kenneth Arrow might have had something similar in mind when he wrote: "The price system is intrinsically limited in scope by our inability to make factual distinctions needed for optimal pricing under uncertainty. Non-market controls, whether internalized as moral principles or externally imposed are to some extent essential for efficiency" (Arrow 1968: 538).

In fact, the rush to remove all impediments to the free functioning of the price system in a vain quest for the illusory rewards of efficiency is actually tearing away some of the forces that have kept the price system from running amok more often. Think, for the moment about the role of the Internet in shopping.

Historically, knowledge, including knowledge about prices, has been costly to obtain. A person would have to devote considerable effort to find out about all the alternative sources of supply. As a result, competition, at least as we have known it in the past, typically did not usually result in uniform prices. For example, George Stigler noted considerable dispersion in prices for identical Chevrolets in Chicago in 1959. Prices varied from $2,350 to $2,515 (Stigler 1961, 214; citing Jung 1960). Stigler acknowledged that different car dealers might have offered different degrees of services or carry a larger range of varieties of stock, but these factors were insufficient to explain such price heterogeneity. Otherwise, why would prices for a homogeneous commodity like anthracite coal in Chicago range from $16.90 to $18.92 (Stigler 1961)?

That dispersion of prices reflected a degree of inertia that helped to buffer the economy. That inertia may be beginning to recede into the past. At least, the visionaries of the so-called "New Information Age" tell us that we are on the threshold of a revolutionary era in which intelligent agents can roam about the Internet collecting information about the prices of various commodities throughout the entire world, let alone the city of Chicago. Should this technology ever come to pass, prices will indeed tend to fall to the level of marginal costs for those goods that are sold competitively. The result will be widespread bankruptcy.

In such a world, business would no longer enjoy the luxury of an installed customer base. Instead, people would instantaneously switch from one supplier to another. While this flexibility would certainly offer immediate advantages for a person who wanted to buy the cheapest commodity today, the result for the economy as a whole would likely be a heightened degree of instability.

Indeed, the one sector where information technology is most advanced is the trading of financial assets. Although financial assets do not bear a large burden of fixed-capital costs, the fruits of this technology seem to be instability. I will return to this subject in my discussion of the instability of foreign currencies.

The Paradox of Market Dynamism

Keynes' vision—that wage and price flexibility might destabilize the economy—requires further comment. As both Keynes and Galbraith believed, the ability of large firms to control their own fate, more or less, stabilized the economy and promoted investment. In contrast, most mainstream economists consider wage and price flexibility to be a positive factor in promoting a healthy economy. Such flexibility supposedly allows the economy to set appropriate prices, which maximize efficiency in the short run, and is an essential factor in making an economy dynamic over a long period.

While both schools of thought shout past one another, each is partially correct. Certainly, rapid adjustment does allow market systems to be more dynamic, especially during booms. Of course, we cannot necessarily credit the dynamism of market societies to the market mechanism. Technological change has been accelerating over the centuries. The emergence of the market may have just happened to have coincided with a cresting of technological capabilities.

Even so, the very survival of the price system ultimately depends, at least to a degree, on the existence of inertia in prices. Where prices react with lightning speed, the forces that Keynes identified can easily push the economy into a depression. Prices, then, must follow another Goldilocks principle: prices must be sufficiently dynamic if the market as a whole is to be dynamic, but not too dynamic, lest the economy spiral out of control. Herein lies the paradox of market dynamism.

In previous centuries, economic behavior was more or less regular. Necessity required that most people work, but custom and tradition limited people's ability to vary their methods of work. The economy may have been unpredictable, but mostly because noneconomic factors, such as the weather, disease, and warfare upset the normal rhythms of economic life.

With the rise of capitalism, new technologies allowed people to lessen the degree to which they were at the mercy of the environment. They could better shelter themselves from the cold. In times of crop failures, improved transportation could bring food from places where the harvest was more plentiful. Although rapid urbanization initially fostered epidemics, later improvements in medicine and sanitation made such outbreaks rarer.

However welcome these technical improvements were, they did not bring economic stability. More and more people found that their livelihood depended upon the capricious changes in fashion.

Credit allowed business to become far more dynamic. A firm no longer had to wait to accumulate funds before it made a major investment. Lenders supposedly had the ability to direct credit to those who were best able to make good use of it.

Credit, however, had another, darker side. As business became more dependent on credit, a new source of instability became more and more common. With an almost pathological regularity, recurrent panics swept across the economy. Again, we find a linking of dynamism and instability.

Anchors Away: The Transformation of the Soviet Economy

The transformation of the Soviet economy to a market economy offers an interesting sidelight on the importance of inertia. Many people expected that the transition to a market economy would bring prosperity to the region within a relatively short period. Although most observers accepted the possibility of a very short term disruption, they expected that the economies of Eastern Europe would get on track without much delay.

Unfortunately, reality was not nearly so generous to the great majority of the people of Eastern Europe. While a select few did become fabulously wealthy, from 1989 to 1994, the gross domestic product in the former Soviet Union fell by an estimated 35 percent. As I mentioned earlier, this collapse was comparable to the Great Depression that the capitalist economies suffered during the 1930s. In 10 of the 15 countries of the Eastern Bloc, the gross domestic product dropped to less than half of its 1989 level (Blanchard and Kremer 1997: 1091).

The standard of living fell in other ways as well. The World Bank, an institution that has always been favorable to the extension of markets, reported: "More Russians are dying during transition. Male life expectancy fell by six years between 1990 and 1994 . . . and that of women by three years. . . . Russian adult mortality is now 10 percent higher than in India" (International Bank for Reconstruction and Development 1996: 128; see also Ellman 1994).

What happened in Eastern Europe reminds us of the importance of long term relations within a market economy. Ralph Hawtrey, perhaps the most distinguished economist in the twentieth century British civil service, once wrote about the long-term:

> Everyone concerned will tend, in the absence of any reason to the contrary, to follow his established routine, and to deal in the way he knows with the people he knows. This continuity in dealings creates what is called business connexion or goodwill. It is the very stuff and substance of the dealer's business. The principal deterrence upon intruders into the market is that they have to create their goodwill from the beginning. The distinguishing characteristic of the successful merchant is the extent and solidity of his goodwill. (Hawtrey 1925: 39)

Although Hawtrey was specifically describing relationships among merchants, he extended his discussion of goodwill to include all sectors of business. Economists never paid any attention to Hawtrey's analysis. As we saw earlier, Ben Bernanke discovered the same principle in the 1980s, when he postulated that depressions are so destructive because they wipe out the basis of banks' long run financial relationships. Olivier Blanchard and Michael Kremer applied the same logic to the Soviet economy, an article entitled, "Disorganization." They contend that once the Soviet economy eliminated most of it long-standing organization of trade and industry, the economy sunk into a morass of confusion from which it still has not recovered (Blanchard and Kremer 1997). Economists are not alone in their recognition of the difficulties in creating markets out of whole cloth. During a visit to Moscow in the spring of 1987, former British prime minister Margaret Thatcher was apparently aware of the impending problems associated with the rapid creation of markets. She warned Mikhail Gorbachev that high officials in the Reagan administration were concerned that *perestroika* was a misstep that threatened to disrupt the workings of the huge Soviet economy. Based on her own difficulties in privatizing industry in Great Britain, she wished the Soviet leader well but warned him to go slow (Dobrynin 1995: 632–3; see also Silk and Silk 1996: 13).

The Russian leadership may have already understood the economic problems with the transition to a market economy. Gorbachev joked about these unnamed "ultraconservative" Americans, but he observed that it would take at least 15 to 20 years to reorganize the Soviet economy. In any case, he never acted on the warning from the Western leaders (Dobrynin 1995: 633). Viktor Chermomyrdin, prime minister under Gorbachev's successor, Boris Yeltsin, offered a glimpse into the reasoning that may have led to the headlong rush into a market economy. He explained bluntly, "Reforms are lethal and that kind of thing cannot he done gradually" (Kagarlitsky 1997: 29). Presumably, Russian leaders were concerned that if the transformation were not presented as a *fait accompli,* the people would recognize the extent of the burden that they would have to bear and thus would resist the change.

According to the theory of markets, such problems should not exist. Alert entrepreneurs should be able to spring into the breach to take advantage of new profit opportunities. The wholesale disruption of the Soviet economy should present an enormous array of potential opportunities that should ensure prosperous times within a brief period.

Unfortunately, upon deeper reflection, the logic of the idea of entrepreneurial alertness assumes that the economy already has a relatively stable structure that enables the entrepreneur to make a fairly well-informed decision. If the economy is in utter disarray, entrepreneurship will be stymied. True, McDonalds and Pizza Huts are springing up in Russia. Many banks and financial institutions are also prospering, but the bones and sinews of a solid economy have been painfully slow in taking shape.

Compare the experience of the former Soviet Union with the quick rebound of the Japanese and the German economies after World War II. Those societies, unlike Russia, could recover so rapidly because they already had a preformed structure around which they could rebuild. In effect, the abandonment of socialism removed too much inertia from the East European economies. In arguing for the importance of inertia, I am not advocating the fossilization of the economy. Certainly, most observers accept that the economies of Eastern Europe could have benefited from the elimination of some inertia. In fact, in some respects excess inertia creates fetters for all economies.

Nonetheless, some degree of inertia is beneficial because it steadies the target so that agents can make relatively informed decisions. Again, I have to appeal to a Goldilocks principle. We want neither too much or too little inertia.

The problem is that we have no quick and easy way of identifying which aspect of economic inertia is excessive and which is insufficient. As Schumpeter noted, cars require both accelerators and brakes to operate safely. However, this observation does little to prevent accidents on the highways. All we can say with confidence is that markets, left to themselves, do not offer enough stability to keep an economy from falling into chaos.

The Instability of Commodity Prices

In 1938, almost a decade after the stock market crash that many believe to have set off the Great Depression, Keynes addressed the instability of the prices of raw materials. Based on this investigation, Keynes concluded: "It is an outstanding fault of the competitive system that there is no sufficient incentive to the individual enterprise to store surplus stocks of materials, so as to maintain continuity of output and to average, as far as possible, periods of high and of low demand. The competitive system abhors the existence of stocks, with as strong a reflex as nature abhors a vacuum, because stocks yield a negative return in terms of themselves" (Keynes 1938: 456–7).

Keynes continued:

> Fluctuations in the prices of the principal raw materials which are produced and marketed in conditions of unrestricted competition, are quite staggering. This is the case not only during well marked trade cycles, but as a result of all sorts of chance causes which lead to fluctuations in immediate demand. The extent of these is apt to be concealed from those who only watch the movements of index numbers and do not study individual commodities; since index numbers, partly by averaging and partly by including many commodities which are not marketed in fully competitive conditions, mask the short-period price fluctuations of the sensitive commodities. (Keynes 1938: 458)

In other words, while a year-to-year index of commodity prices might not show a great deal of instability, within any given year prices of individual commodities might fluctuate wildly. To prove his point, Keynes analyzed the price movements of four commodities (rubber, cotton, wheat, and lead). In the case of rubber, he found "There has only been one year in the last ten in which the high price of the year has exceeded the low by less than 70 per cent. The average excess of the year's high over the year's low has been 96 per cent. In other words, there is on the average some date in every year in which the price of rubber is approximately double its price at some other date in that year" (Keynes 1938: 458).

The fluctuations of cotton prices, although less extreme, still gave no comfort to those who harbor a belief in the natural stability of markets. Keynes found: "Only twice in the last ten years has the high price [of cotton] of the year exceeded the low by less than 33 per cent and the average excess of the year's high over the year's low has been 42 per cent" (Keynes 1938: 458).

For the four commodities as a whole, the average annual variation in the ten previous years between the lowest and the highest prices in the same year was 67 percent.

During the early years following the end of World War II, international arrangements, known as the Bretton Woods agreements, stabilized the value of the major currencies, partly following Keynes' recommendation. The Bretton Woods regime dampened the wild swings in commodity prices until the system broke down in the early 1970s. Then, price instability in raw materials became common once again. One study estimated that after 1971, extent of price fluctuations became four to five times higher than they were under the period of managed currencies (Sylos-Labini 1982: 150).

Speculation and Economic Stability

Not surprisingly, many conservative economists opposed Bretton Woods. After all, most laissez-faire economists consider sticky wages or anything else that interferes with the free workings of the market to be a source of inefficiency. The market, they tell us, will automatically provide both stability and efficiency. Anything that stands in the way of the free functioning of the market will be detrimental to society as a whole.

A case in point was supposed to be the market for foreign exchange. First, some brief background. Following the disruption associated with the Great Depression, many economists came to the conclusion that the irrational behavior that drives the foreign exchange markets contributed to the instability of economies around the world (Nurkse 1944; and Krugman 1989: 79). This perspective led to the Bretton Woods agreement to manage foreign exchange rates so as to cushion economies from instability originating outside their borders.

Milton Friedman was the most forceful opponent of this arrangement. He insisted that efforts to attempt to maintain a fixed price for a currency were futile. Governments were unable to keep their currency overvalued or undervalued for an extended period. Sooner or later, currency values would have to conform to market fundamentals.

The expression "market fundamentals" refers to the underlying economic forces that supposedly would unerringly drive the economy along a successful equilibrium path if only governments refrain from meddling in economic affairs. Although even highly intelligent individuals might be mistaken about fundamentals, supposedly the market as a whole will not be misled.

Friedman concluded that governments should let the market determine the appropriate price of the currency rather than attempt to control the value of foreign currency. Speculators would bring order to the market for foreign exchange, since a rational trader would sell when prices are high and buy when prices are low. In Friedman's words: "People who have argued that speculation can be destabilizing seldom realize that this is largely equivalent to saying that speculators lose money, since speculation can be destabilizing in general only if speculators sell when the currency is low in price and buy when it is high" (Friedman 1953b: 175).

In this way, speculators, by eliminating the peaks and valleys of price fluctuations, would supposedly make the system more stable. According to Friedman, inept speculators who fail to understand market conditions eventually have to leave the market. As a result, the pool of speculators remaining in the market would be the ones who would have the expertise to narrow the range of price fluctuation. For this reason, Friedman insisted that speculation would work to contain price fluctuations, ensuring stability in foreign exchange markets.

In 1939, Nicholas Kaldor, a distinguished economist from Cambridge University, published an important article that anticipated Friedman's theory and put it in context. In the process, Kaldor made the three points that Friedman had overlooked (Kaldor 1939). First, Kaldor noted that speculation will tend to narrow the range of price fluctuations only when speculators have a limited effect on the total price. Second, speculators could keep a step ahead of the market in one of two ways. Either speculators would have to have the capacity to understand the fundamentals of the market or they could merely exercise their ability to predict the actions of other speculators. In the latter case, speculation will be likely to exacerbate price fluctuations (Kaldor 1939: 18–19). Third, Kaldor pointed out that even if speculation were successful in limiting price stability, the actions of speculators might still make output more unstable (Kaldor 1939: 19).

Finally, Kaldor noted that the belief that the future supply price will not differ much from past prices will be stronger, the more money wages are stable: "It is in this way that the rigidity of money wages contributes to the stability of the economic system, by inducing the forces of speculation to operate in a much more stabilizing fashion" (Kaldor 1939: 35).

In other words, pure market forces have the tendency to run amok; however, stable wages might provide a modest anchor that would allow the system to enjoy relative stability, as Keynes had observed only a few years before Kaldor (Keynes 1936). In the absence of this anchor, speculation would be more likely to destabilize prices. We could rephrase Kaldor's conclusion by stating that market forces will be more effective in stabilizing markets in an environment in which market forces are constrained; that is, where institutional forces tend to make wages relatively stable or reduce the ability of speculators to move prices radically.

A casual look at the workings of the economy seems to bear out Kaldor's idea. Where pure market forces are more free to work, price movements are more extreme and show little relationship to economic fundamentals. The foreign exchange market seems to be a case in point.

The Instability of International Financial Markets

By 1973, Milton Friedman's long-time objective of a free market in foreign exchange came to pass as the Bretton Woods agreement unraveled. This new environment put Friedman's ideas to the test. Financial markets rather than governments got to determine the value of currencies in international markets. Indeed, the foreign exchange market became one of the purest markets ever to exist:

> As of mid-1989, the average volume of trading activity (adjusted for double counting) was about $430 billion per day. To get a sense for just how big this number is, consider that daily U.S. GNP is about $22 billion, and daily world trade in goods and services is about $11 billion. Since foreign exchange trading is so much greater in volume than is trade in real goods and services, foreign exchange markets would seem to be highly liquid and efficient. (Froot and Thaler 1990: 180)

By 1995, average daily foreign exchange trading soared to $1.260 trillion, and the ratio of foreign exchange trading to world trade was nearly 70:1. The total value of the entire holdings of gold and foreign exchange held by the world's central banks was $1.500 trillion, which was slightly more than one day's worth of foreign exchange trading (Palley 1998: 178).

This enormous market works with virtually no regulation. Traders freely move billions of dollars worth of currencies with a few keystrokes. If any market should be efficient, it should be this one. The result of this experiment, however, has not been a happy one for those who believe in the magic of the marketplace.

Although floating exchange rates were predicted to move smoothly, after 1973, they have in fact moved erratically and often with little relation to fundamentals (Helleiner 1994: 122). As Paul Krugman has noted: "Never before has there been such extraordinary instability of exchange rates in the absence of very high inflation. . . . At the very least, we have to say that the evidence offers no positive support for the view that the foreign-exchange market is an efficient information processor" (Krugman 1989: 1, 87).

More recently, Krugman has suggested that exchange rates might be even more unstable in the absence of the cost associated with foreign currency transactions. In his words: "It may be small frictions that prevent a subjectively low-probability crisis from ballooning into a full-fledged speculative attack. If this is true, then the improving technical efficiency of markets may actually be a contributory factor to the frequency of currency crises in the 1990s" (Krugman 1997).

Even with the benefit of hindsight, economists have not been able to find any convincing way to explain foreign exchange prices in terms of any economic fundamentals. For example, between 1980 and 1985, the value of the dollar relative to an index of G-10 currencies rose from about 88 to about 145 (Palley 1998: 148). Although economists had no difficulty in explaining the soaring value of the dollar in terms of their own perception of fundamentals, they could not agree on just what these fundamentals were.

Some said that investors expected future appreciation of the dollar; others said that dollar investments would be increasingly profitable relative to assets in other countries; still others said that assets in the United States were less risky than elsewhere (Froot and Frankel 1986: 24).

Even though advocates of each approach found confirmation for their pet theories in this rise in the dollar, the dollar continued its rise well after it had adjusted to the supposed underlying fundamentals (Froot and Frankel 1986: 25). An exasperated Federal Reserve economist suggested that we follow the strategy of the hypothetical lazy weather forecaster discussed in the Chapter 1: "Exchange rates don't seem to be affected by economic fundamentals in the short run. Being able to predict money supplies, central bank policies, or other supposed influences doesn't help forecast the exchange rate. Economists have found instead that the best forecast of the exchange rate, at least in the short-run, is whatever it happens to be today" (Hopper 1997: 17).

Nonetheless, despite Friedman's unwarranted confidence in markets, the most important influence on foreign exchange rates seems to be sentiment, ungrounded in any economic fundamentals. So, in conclusion, the experience of the foreign exchange markets lends support to my thesis that the absence of instability in markets owes a great deal to the existence of nonmarket forces. When we remove these supposed impediments to markets, as we did in the case of the foreign exchange markets, we find a marked increase in volatility, if not outright instability.

Economic Integration and Instability

Ecologists have long known that a more diverse habitat tends to be more stable. A weak connectivity between species helps to protect ecological systems from collapse or explosion (Louca 1997: 206).

Agricultural systems illustrate how homogeneity can open a system up to threats. For example, primitive agricultural communities protect themselves by planting a wide diversity of plants. One kind of corn might do better in a dry year; another, in a wet season. In this way, farmers gave themselves a form of insurance.

In the United States, seed companies bred virtually all the hybrid corn with a single gene, Texas Male Sterile, to save the cost of hiring about 125,000 high school students to cut the tassels off the breeding stock. This same gene made the corn particularly susceptible to a strain of a fungus disease. Nobody realized how this gene weakened the corn until 1970, when an outbreak wiped out 43 percent of the crop in South Carolina. The agricultural sector feared that comparable losses were possible across the nation, but a favorable weather pattern held the losses to 15 percent for the nation (Perelman 1977: 47).

Since the degree integration of the world financial markets is such a new phenomenon, we do not have much experience in this regard. The agricultural analogy represents a useful warning rather than a scientific analysis of the integration of world financial markets.

My instincts do suggest to me that the dangers of a contagion of panic are greater now than ever before with the ever-tightening links among world financial markets. A breakdown in any one location may be more likely to spread across the globe than ever before. At the time of the writing of this book, as the worsening economic crisis in Asia threatens to undermine the economies of Russia and Brazil, we can get a glimpse at how a global breakdown could unfold.

For example, historically, the people of poor nations that produced primary products absorbed part of the financial shocks that hit the advanced economies (Patnaik 1997: 9). Today, these same poor nations are integrated within the international financial system. Shocks that hit these nations reverberate back on the international financial system, perhaps even exacerbating the initial shock.

If I am correct, then, the need for inertia to protect the economy may also be more pressing than ever before.

The Need for Sand in Gears

About the time that the Bretton Woods agreement dissolved, James Tobin suggested that international financial markets were too efficient in their ability to respond to perceived changes in the market. He proposed a tax, now known as the "Tobin tax," on such transactions to "throw sand in the gears" of the system (Tobin 1974: 88).

A few years later, Tobin repeated his proposal "to throw some sand into the wheels of our excessively efficient money markets" (Tobin 1978: 154). He admitted that his earlier call "fell like a stone in a deep well" (Tobin 1978: 155). Even so, Tobin held firm to his view that something needed to be done to create some sort of inertia. He insisted: "I must remain skeptical that the price signals that the unanchored markets give are signals that will guide economies to their true comparative advantage, capital to its efficient international allocation and governments to correct macroeconomic policies" (Tobin 1978: 158).

Tobin's suggestion was not altogether original. Four decades earlier, before the creation of the Bretton Woods agreement, Keynes had made a similar suggestion: "The introduction of a substantial Government transfer tax on all transactions might prove the most serviceable reform available, with a view to mitigating the predominance of speculation over enterprise in the United States" (Keynes 1936: 160).

My perspective is not as measured as that of either Tobin or Keynes. I do not believe that the question is whether or not price signals are efficient indicators of correct economic policy. I believe that a purely competitive price system has an inherent tendency to spin out of control; that the anchors to which Tobin alluded are what prevents this instability from being more pervasive.

True, the small tax rate that Tobin proposed, however, is far too small an anchor to stem the tide of massive flows of speculative capital. For example, Paul Davidson notes that when "the Mexican peso fell by approximately 60 percent in the Winter of 1994–5, [a] Tobin tax of over 23 percent would have been required to stop the speculative surge of the Peso crisis" (Davidson 1977: 678).

Nonetheless, Tobin's instincts were correct. A quick response to changing information can indeed create instability. Recall the earlier example of the difficulty of adjusting the temperature of water while taking a shower. In the shower, rapid reactions can make the system become unstable. When the water initially comes out too cold, we turn up the temperature. The water may still be too cold, so we turn up the heat some more, not realizing that if we waited a bit more, the water would soon reach the desired temperature. Because we did not realize about the build up of hot water that was in motion, we turn the temperature up again, making the water unbearably hot. So we turn the temperature down, repeating the process in reverse. Each time we overshoot, we may overreact, resulting in an overshooting in the opposite direction. Had we reacted more slowly, we might have had an easier time adjusting the temperature.

Researchers have been exploring the properties of economies where computers would allow speculators to make lightening-quick decisions. The evidence so far suggests that such economies would be disastrously unstable. One researcher compared such economies to a car travelling 500 miles an hour (Ward 1998).

Rational people can avoid the problem by stepping out of the shower after the water becomes uncomfortably hot or uncomfortably cold. We do not have an easy method to step out of an economy. For that reason, we can benefit from institutions, regulations, or conventions that make the system less flexible.

Forces for Instability

The forces that make for economic instability are numerous and wide-ranging. Natural disasters, war, and other catastrophes can all destabilize an economy. Technical change and innovation can also upset the existing order, as Schumpeter emphasized. Speculation and lack of coordination add a further element of instability, as we repeatedly find in the works of Keynes.

At the same time, economic adjustments can act as a shock absorber, reducing the dislocation associated with the sorts of changes that we discussed above. For example, a shortage of one material sets off a surge of efforts to find an alternative. In this sense, the conservative case for markets is at its strongest.

The difficulty comes when we try to reconcile the two conflicting theories of market flexibility. While market flexibility acts as a buffer to reduce economic shocks, the same flexibility also induces instability into the economy.

Here we come back again to the sort of debates that we encountered in discussing Friedman's theory of foreign exchange markets. As Kaldor had suggested, to the extent that the market flexibility responds to economic fundamentals, we might expect that flexibility would contribute to stability. To the extent that financial conditions feed on themselves, flexibility is liable to destabilize the economy.

Of course, nobody has been able to explain just what market fundamentals are. Moreover, as Karl Polanyi insisted, labor, land, and money are not produced as commodities. Only because we are accustomed to treating them as such do they seem to be like other commodities. For such fictitious commodities, market fundamentals are illusory, at best.

We can rephrase Polanyi's point in a slightly different fashion by thinking of the conventional picture of the market as a feedback mechanism. Most theories of economic stability depend on some sort of feedback mechanism. For example, if the demand for cars goes up, short run shortages may appear, signaling producers to manufacture more cars. If the cost of producing cars increases and prices rise, consumers will probably ration their purchases of new cars. Ultimately, this feed-back system revolves around the cost of reproducing commodities.

Polanyi understood that these fictitious commodities—land, labor, and money—are not produced like real commodities. As a result, the feedback mechanisms required for stability are absent.

This idea returns us to Keynes' observations about the importance of price anchors. Without feedback from the cost of production, financial speculation can move the prices of these fictitious commodities almost without bounds. For this reason, Keynes seems to lead us to the conclusion that we largely owe what economic stability that we enjoy to forces other than those of laissez-faire, whether these forces of inertia be resistance of labor to rapid decreases in wages, the monopolistic powers of large corporations, or government regulation.

Although Keynes was socially conservative, his economic theory demanded a radical break with the traditional method of doing economics. Few of Keynes' would-be disciples were wholly prepared to throw all of their old economics overboard. Instead, they reinterpreted Keynes in a way that was consistent with their traditional training, forgetting Keynes' insights about the importance of anchors.

The Rise of the New Keynesians

The most popular variant of Keynesian economics was Paul Samuelson's famous neoclassical synthesis (Samuelson 1955). According to this safe but desiccated version of Keynes, the economy works just fine, except that it requires a bit of a nudge by way of monetary or fiscal policy in order to move it toward full employment. As this brand of "Keynesian" economics fell into disrepute during the economic crises of the late 1970s, a school of economists proclaiming themselves "New Keyensian economists" began to spring up.

According to the economics of the New Keynesians, even the mild macropolicies of the neoclassical synthesis fell from view. Instead, they emphasized that the economy might not reach an equilibrium, but only because of economic rigidities, such as the unwillingness of labor to accept cuts in wages, together with some problems in getting adequate information (Greenwald and Stiglitz 1993). The economy lacked only a few microeconomic adjustments to perform optimally.

In truth, the New Keynesians were hardly Keynesian at all. As we already saw, Keynes regarded rigidities as preventing instability rather than hindering a movement toward a full-employment equilibrium. True,

Keynes never went into great depth about his analysis of anchors. Gardiner Means once asked Keynes outright if his analysis depended on an assumption of rigid prices or wages. Keynes responded categorically, "Not at all" (Goode 1994: 179).

Although wage and price rigidities were not at the core of Keynes' theory, the New Keynesian economists treated them as if they were the centerpiece of his analysis. In addition, the New Keynesians concentrate their analysis on measures designed to get the economy back to an equilibrium position.

Instead, Keynes saw the Depression as an equilibrium, albeit an undesirable one. He was groping for a way to get the economy back toward full employment. However, unlike the New Keynesians who design modest measures, Keynes recognized that only massive changes in economic policy could defeat the Depression. Although Keynes never succeeded in formulating what these policies might be, he gave no evidence whatsoever that the feeble microeconomic policies of the New Keynesians could in any way be relevant.

New Keynesianism might not be Keynesian, but it had other attractions. This theory offered a way to look at the economy that was both comfortable and respectable. The New Keynesians did not have to adopt the ridiculous notion that the market is perfect, yet they could still base their theory on the notion of an equilibrium. Rather than risk becoming marginalized by adopting a heretical position about the economy, they contented themselves with merely allowing a single rigidity or a solitary lapse in the process of generating information. Within this framework, a clever economist can easily manufacture a sophisticated mathematical model of how the economy could achieve an equilibrium, while taking pride on interjecting a note of realism into an otherwise sterile economic theory.

This sort of analysis played right into the hands of those who maintained that disequilibrium was the result of intransigent labor rather than a characteristic of the system as a whole. Supposedly, if wages were not so "sticky," then the system could operate smoothly, ignoring the problems of information.

The New Keynesian school sees itself as opposing the simple-minded notion that economies automatically move toward an equilibrium, but Keynes' embryonic ideas on wage rigidity went much further than the New Keynesians. In fact, we saw that Keynes identified the very ideas that the New Keynesians would later embrace with the old economists whose ideas he was attempting to overturn.

The Subjectivity of Keynesian Economics

In one sense, the New Keynesians seem to have a valid claim to follow in the footsteps of Keynes. Both Keynes and the New Keynesians insist that the credit system does not operate perfectly. Keynes' interpretation of the problem, however, is considerably different from that of the New Keynesians. For the New Keynesians, the credit system malfunctions when some shock, such as a depression, interferes with the smooth transmission of adequate information or when agents are unable to assess the intentions of others. For Keynes, however, the concept of adequate information had no meaning whatsoever. The credit system depends upon people's intuition concerning the future state of the economy as a whole.

Nobody has any way of knowing what the future holds. We can guess; we can rely on conventions; or we can just continue to do tomorrow what we did yesterday. But in no case can we have adequate information about the future. Alas, uncertainty rather than information pervades Keynes' world.

Given this uncertainty, information cascades can occur. A small, even insignificant, event can trigger massive changes in market sentiment. A single bankruptcy or even a rumor can expose preexisting doubts about the economy. Suddenly, everybody tries to sell ahead of the crowd, setting off a panic. How can you explain this train of events in a simple mathematical form? Even the complex and inelegant mathematics of fluid dynamics will be inadequate.

Realizing the inherent instability of the system—even though this subject was not at the center of his *General Theory*—Keynes called for a substantial transfer tax to throw sand in the gears of the economy.

Keynes' emphasis on uncertainty makes Keynes' economics, as opposed to New Keynesianism, unattractive to most economists. Economists need to assume a degree of certainty in order to be able to work with equations that they can solve mathematically or to obtain novel statistical results. When the whole economy turns on the subjective state of all the participants, all the pretty little graphs or equations do not have any relevance. In effect, then, Keynes' approach wipes out much of the value of conventional economic training.

Interesting enough, Keynes' most formidable rivals among conventional economists, members of the Austrian school of economics also emphasize subjectivity, like Keynes. We might expect that the Austrian school would enjoy a massive following. After all, the Austrians are fervid believers in laissez-faire in an age when laissez-faire theory is popular. Nonetheless, the

Austrian school can muster only a tiny but growing group of adherents, despite considerable financial support from foundations that appreciate their defense of laissez-faire. I suspect that their radical subjectivity lies at the heart of their lack of popularity.

CHAPTER 10

Loose Threads

A Brief Digression on Intellectual Property

While the thrust of economic policy over the past few decades has been to whittle away those features of the economy that slow down markets and create inertia, we have yet to address one glaring exception: the formation of intellectual property rights. At first glance, you might think that the creation of intellectual property rights might be in line with the marketization of all aspects of life. In fact, in a sense, it is perhaps the most extreme example of marketization—that ideas and thoughts become ordinary commodities, much like radios or canned food.

Intellectual property differs from other commodities in a number of important respects (Perelman 1998); first and foremost, intellectual property rights convey monopoly power to their owner. The law forbids me to make a Microsoft Word program, a Mickey Mouse wristwatch, or a shoe with a Nike "swoosh," unless, of course, I first get permission from the owners of these intellectual property rights.

By conferring an absolute monopoly to those holding intellectual property rights, the law prevents the tendency to the sort of deflationary pressure that burdens ordinary markets. During the 1980s, when the software industry was still immature, after a company built up a dominant position, it was not immune from competitive pressure. However, the corporate decline in this industry was different from what other industries typically experienced. These firms tended to shrink into insignificance or even disappear within a very short time. We might even think about our image of evolution during the Cambrian explosion when contemplating the early history of the software industry.

For example, Wordstar was once the dominant word-processing program. The company that owned the program failed to make improvements in its product fast enough. The program expired in short order. Its successor, WordPerfect, still exists, although the company that produced it has been bought out, and the market share of the program is small. Today, Microsoft controls the market for word processing, spreadsheets, operating systems, and much else in the world of software. Because of the highly integrated nature of Microsoft's product, even if a rival firm produced a superior word-processing program or spreadsheet, it would have difficulty in displacing Microsoft's version.

At this point, I am at a loss to predict the future of the industry. Will Microsoft be able to retain its dominance for long? Will government regulation or new technology succeed in dislodging the company? We can only speculate.

What we can say for sure is that our knowledge of economics is ill suited to such situations. More to the point, the intellectual property rights of a company such as Microsoft does create substantial inertia. Whether it will stabilize or fossilize the economy is an open question.

Simulated Competition and Inertia

Earlier, in Chapter 7, I discussed the notion of simulated competition, whereby higher wages or more effective environmental regulation would force business to discover superior technologies. How does the strategy of simulated competition fit in with ideas about inertia that I have been proposing? Recall Schumpeter's notion that major technological innovations are, per se, destabilizing. Could the promotion of simulated competition represent a diminution of beneficial inertia?

Institutions that create inertia can also provide what the German sociologist, Wolfgang Streeck, called "beneficial constraints." He offers several examples to illustrate his point. According to Streeck, the legal protection of artisanal firms in Germany in the late nineteenth century helped preserve the apprenticeship system, thereby contributing to German economic performance and competitiveness in later years (Streeck 1997, p. 211). In addition, he noted:

> whereas German institutional rigidities have largely foreclosed adjustment to price-competitive markets, they have at the same time and instead forced, induced and enabled managements to embark on more demanding high value-added, diversified quality production strategies. While making structural

> adjustment and the maintenance of competitiveness more difficult, German institutions have not made it impossible, and indeed they seem to have made more difficult adjustment strategies more possible. (Streeck 1997, 31)

In Chapter 7, I also proposed that a sequence of dramatic technological improvements during the late nineteenth century was in fact destabilizing. Increasing demand subsequent to the Civil War and increasing scale thanks to the enormous improvements in transportation seem to have encouraged the adoption of these technologies, although at an early stage in this development, high wages for skilled workers may well have played a role.

Of course, inertia as such is not a basic social goal. Inertia serves a purpose only insofar as it keeps markets from spinning out of control. Even so, could the simulated competition of high wages create a cascade of new technologies capable of creating instability?

In Chapter 7, I also proposed that a sequence of dramatic technological improvements during the late nineteenth century was in fact destabilizing. Increasing demand subsequent to the Civil War and increasing scale thanks to the enormous improvements in transportation seem to have been the root causes of the adoption of these technologies, although at an early stage in this development, high wages for skilled workers may well have played a role.

However, as the new technologies took hold, they dampened the pressure for high wages. If a high-wage policy had remained in effect, the extra payments to labor might well have offset the destabilizing influence of new technology. Admittedly, the experience of one period does not rule out the possibility that high wages could set off a destabilizing round of innovations, but it might suggest why such destabilization might be unlikely.

Economics vs. Nature

So far, for the most part, I have treated natural processes as a metaphor for economic processes. Within this perspective, I have treated such processes as if they were somehow self-contained, separate from the influence of human activity. At several points in the preceding chapters, I also noted that the economy was unlike nature because humans created the market.

In reality, nothing could be more untrue. Natural processes and economic processes are intimately related. We are actively engaged in reshaping nature. In some cases, the goal is to modify nature directly. We dam up rivers and level hills. In other cases, the effects are unintentional, as when we set toxins loose on the environment with no idea about what their ultimate effect will be.

Many natural processes are unable to survive the barrage of shocks that the economy has unleashed on the environment; hence, I must modify another earlier remark that I made solely for the purpose of argument: I must retract the distinction that I made between the frequency of economic crises and mass extinctions.

While earlier periods of mass extinctions may been separated by many millennia, presently, the earth is witnessing a mass extinction of perhaps unprecedented proportions. At least one of every eight plant species in the world—and nearly one of three in the United States—is under threat of extinction, according to the first comprehensive worldwide assessment of plant endangerment (Stevens 1998). Unlike business cycles, which eventually lay the groundwork for the subsequent revival, the present mass extinction shows no sign of reversing itself.

According to the Harvard biologist Edward O. Wilson, one of the world's leading authorities on biodiversity, the extinction of species is now occurring at the staggering rate of 27,000 species a year—74 every day, three every hour. Wilson estimates that up to 20 percent of the world's species could become extinct over the next three decades, a rate of extinction not experienced since the disappearance of the dinosaurs 65 million years ago (Foster 1997: 126; citing Wilson 1992: 278–80).

The continuing collapse of natural processes threatens to undermine the basis of our economy. Environmental protection might create inertia with respect to protection of the natural habitat, although success in this matter is far from guaranteed. All too often, what we do to preserve nature from one danger only diverts us into doing something even more destructive. For example, when the government banned the pesticide DDT, industry did not look to alternatives to pesticides. Instead, it induced industry to substitute even more deadly chemicals.

High wages can have an ambiguous effect on the environment. More affluent people ostensibly put a higher value on natural amenities than those who are more economically constrained, but they also consume more goods than their less fortunate brethren. All too often, they resolve this contradiction by watching environmentally destructive activities be displaced to locations where poorer people reside.

A high-wage economy could possibly turn to consuming fewer goods and more services. Perhaps computerization could offset energy intensive activities, as is the case in telecommuting. Unfortunately, the grounds for such speculation are not very solid.

Conclusion

I have been making the case that competition has a tendency to spin out of control. Thanks to a combination of good fortune and a residue of customs, institutions, and practices, we have not yet witnessed a reprise of the Great Depression. All the while, our leaders are hell bent on whittling away these protective measures that slow down economic responses enough so that we have been able to enjoy relative economic stability over the past few decades.

We are running an enormous risk by experimenting with the economy without taking into account the dangers we face by removing the very forces that have provided a modicum of protection to the economy. Of course, "protectionism," as that word is used in debates about international trade policy, has a bad ring to it.

I have also made the case that we should go farther in instituting other measures that might resemble protectionism in a broader sense—policies to increase wages or protect the environment. In actual fact, these policies, rather than curtailing competition, simulate the positive aspects of competition, while avoiding some of the negative repercussions.

I do not pretend that creating inertia will make markets perform perfectly, or even well. My only point is that inertia can make markets perform better.

As I suggested in the last chapter, "Loose Threads," I bring more questions than answers. In an age where arrogant self-confidence is the norm in economic debates, we will do well to be more open to questions.

References

Abernathy, William J., and Utterback, James M. 1978. "Patterns of Industrial Innovation." *Technology Review* (June/July): 41–7.

Adams, Charles Francis. 1876. "The State and the Railroad," Pts. 1–2. *Atlantic Monthly* (March): 360–70, and (June): 691–9.

Akerlof, George, William Dickens, and George Perry. 1996. "The Macroeconomics of Low Inflation." *Brookings Papers on Economic Activity,* No. 1: 1–60.

Aldcroft, Derek H. 1983. *The British Economy Between the Wars.* Oxford: Philip Allen, 74–5.

Amsden, Alice H. 1989. *Asia's Next Giant: South Korea and Late Industrialization.* New York: Oxford University Press.

Amsden, Jon, and Brier, Stephen. 1977. "Coal Miners on Strike: The Transformation of Strike Demands and the Formation of a National Union in the U.S. Coal Industry, 1881–1894." *Journal of Interdisciplinary History* (Spring): 583–616.

Anderson, Lisa R., and Charles A. Holt. 1997. "Information Cascades in the Laboratory." *American Economic Review,* Vol. 87, No. 4 (December): 847–63.

———. 1968. "The Economics of Moral Hazard: A Further Comment." *American Economic Review,* Vol. 58, No. 3 (June): 537–9.

Arrow, Kenneth J. 1992. "I Know a Hawk from a Handsaw." In M. Szenberg, ed., *Eminent Economists: Their Life and Philosophies.* Cambridge: Cambridge University Press, 42–50.

Arthur, W. Brian. 1989. "Competing Technologies, Increasing Returns, and Lock-in by Historical Events." *Economic Journal,* Vol. 99, No. 394 (March): 116–31.

Atack, Jeremy. 1986. "Firm Size and Industrial Structure in the United States during the Nineteenth Century." *Journal of Economic History,* Vol. 46, No. 2 (June): 463–75.

Audretsch, David B. 1995. *Innovation and Industry Evolution.* Cambridge: MIT Press.

Audretsch, David B., and Zoltan J. Acs. 1994. "Entrepreneurial Activity, Innovation, and Macroeconomic Fluctuations." In Yuichi Shionoya and Mark Perlman, eds. *Innovation in Technology, Industries, and Institutions: Studies in Schumpeterian Perspectives.* Ann Arbor: University of Michigan Press: 173–83.

Bagehot, Walter. 1873. *Lombard Street.* Homewood, Ill: Richard D. Irwin.

Baily, Martin Neil. 1995. "Efficiency in Manufacturing and the Need for Global Competition." *Brookings Papers on Economic Activity: Microeconomics,* 307–47.

Baird, Bruce C. 1997. "Necessity and the 'Perverse' Supply of Labor in Pre-Classical British Political Economy." *History of Political Economy,* Vol. 29, No. 3 (Fall): 497–522.

Barkai, Haim, 1993. "Productivity Patterns, Exchange Rates and the Gold Standard Restoration Debate of the 1920s." *History of Political Economy,* Vol. 25, No. 1 (Spring): 1–38.

Beesley, M. E., and R. T. Hamilton. 1984. "Small Firms' Seedbed Role and the Concept of Turbulence." *Journal of Industrial Economics,* Vol. 33, No. 2 (December): 217–31.

Bernanke, Ben S. 1981. "Bankruptcy, Liquidity, and Recession." *American Economic Review,* Vol. 71, No. 2 (May), 155–9.

———. 1983. "Nonmonetary Effects of the Financial Crisis in the Propagation of the Great Depression." *American Economic Review,* Vol. 73, No. 3 (June): 257–76.

Blanchard, Olivier, and Michael Kremer. 1997. "Disorganization." *Quarterly Journal of Economics,* Vol. 112, No. 4 (November): 1091–1126.

Bluestone, Barry. 1988. "Deindustrialization and Unemployment in America." *Review of Black Political Economy,* Vol. 17, No. 2 (Fall): 29–44.

Bluestone, Barry and Harrison, Bennett. 1982. *The Deindustrialization of America: Plant Closings, Community Abandonment, and the Dismantling of Basic Industry.* New York: Basic Books.

Boianovsky, Mauro. 1995. "Wicksell's Business Cycle." *European Journal of the History of Economic Thought,* Vol. 2, No. 2 (Autumn): 375–411.

Boswell, James. 1934. *Life of Johnson,* Oxford: Clarendon Press, 6 vols. G. B. Hill, ed., 85–6.

Bourgin, Frank. 1989. *The Great Challenge: The Myth of Laissez-Faire in the Early Republic.* New York: Harper and Row Publishers.

Bresnahan, Timothy F., and Daniel M. G. Raff. 1991. "Intra-Industry Heterogeneity and the Great Depression: The American Motor Vehicles Industry, 1929–1935." *Journal of Economic History,* Vol. 51, No. 1 (March): 317–31.

Brown, Gardner M., Jr. 1990. "Valuation of Genetic Resources." In Gordon H. Orians et al., eds. *The Preservation and Valuation of Biological Resources.* Seattle: University of Washington Press: 203–29.

Buchanan, James M., and Richard E. Wagner. 1977. *Democracy in Deficit.* New York: Academic Press.

Carter, Anne P. 1970. *Structural Change in the American Economy.* Cambridge: Harvard University Press.

Caves, Richard E. 1977. *American Industry: Structure, Conduct, Performance.* 4th ed. Englewood Cliffs, N. J.: Prentice-Hall.

———. 1980. "The Structure of Industry." In Martin Feldstein, ed., *The American Economy in Transition: A Sixtieth Anniversary Conference.* Chicago: University of Chicago Press, 501–44.

Churchill, Winston. 1927. "Letter to Sir Richard Hopkins, 22 July." In Martin Gilbert, ed., *Winston S. Churchill.* Vol. 5, *The Exchequer Years 1922–1929 and the*

Wilderness Years 1929–1935, Pts. 1 and 2 Boston: Houghton Mifflin, 1981: i, 1310–1.

Clark, Victor Selden. 1929. *History of Manufactures in the United States.* 3 vols. Vol. 1. *1607–1860.* New York: McGraw-Hill.

Comanor, William S., and F. M. Scherer. 1995. "Rewriting History: The Early Sherman Act Monopolization Cases." *Journal of Business Economics,* Vol. 2, No. 2: 263–89.

Cooke, Frederick H. 1893. "Industrial Depressions: Their Causes and Cures." *American Journal of Politics,* Vol. 3 (December): 597–604.

Cusumano, Michael A., Yiorgos Mylonadis, and Richard S. Rosenbloom. 1992. "Strategic Maneuvering and Mass-Market Dynamics: The Triumph of VHS over Beta." *Business History Review,* Vol. 66, No. 1 (Spring): 51–94.

Dalton, George. 1982. "Barter." *Journal of Economic Issues,* Vol. 16, No, 1 (March): 181–91.

Danhof, Clarence. 1941. "Farm Making Costs and the 'Safety Valve.'" *Journal of Political Economy,* Vol. 49, No. 3 (June): 217–59.

Darwin, Charles. 1964. *On the Origin of Species.* Cambridge: Harvard University Press.

Davidson, Paul. 1997. "Are Grains of Sand in the Wheels of International Finance Sufficient to Do the Job When Boulders Are Often Required?" *Economic Journal,* Vol. 107, No. 442 (May): 671–86.

Dean, J. W., and Mark Perlman. 1998. "Harvey Leibenstein as a Pioneer of Our Time." *Economic Journal,* Vol. 108, No. 446 (January): 132–52.

De Long, J. Bradford. 1990. "Did J. P. Morgan's Men Add Value? An Historical Perspective on Financial Market Innovation." In Peter Temin, ed. 1991. *Inside the Business Enterprise: The Use and Transformation of Information.* Chicago: University of Chicago Press, 205–36.

Desimone, Livio D., and Frank Popoff. 1997. *Eco-Efficiency: The Business Link to Sustainable Development.* Cambridge: MIT Press.

Dobrynin, Anatoly. 1995. *In Confidence: Moscow's Ambassador to America's Six Cold War Presidents, 1962–1986.* New York: Times Books.

Donaldson, Gordon. 1984. *Managing Corporate Wealth.* New York: Praeges.

Durocher, Leo Ernest. 1975. *Nice Guys Finish Last.* New York: Simon and Schuster.

Edwards, Rick. 1975. "Stages in Corporate Stability and the Risks of Corporate Failure." *Journal of Economic History,* Vol. 35, No. 2 (June): 428–60.

Egnal, Marc. 1996. *Divergent Paths: How Culture and Institutions Have Shaped North American Growth.* New York: Oxford University Press.

Ehrlich, Paul R., and Anne H. Ehrlich. 1996. *Betrayal of Science and Reason: How Anti-environmental Rhetoric Threatens Our Future.* Washington, D.C.: Island Press.

Einzig, Paul. 1966. *Primitive Money: Its Ethnological, Historical and Economic Aspects.* 2d ed. Oxford: Pergamon Press.

Ellman, Michael. 1994. "The Increase in Death and Disease under 'Katastroika.'" *Cambridge Journal of Economics,* Vol. 18, No. 4 (August): 329–55.

Enthoven, Alain C. 1963. "Economic Analysis in the Department of Defense." *American Economic Review,* Vol. 53, No. 2 (May): 413–23.

Etzioni, Amitai. 1988. *The Moral Dimension: Toward a New Economics.* New York: Free Press.

Ferri, Piero, and Hyman P. Minsky. 1991. "Market Processes and Thwarting Systems." Jerome Levy Economics Institute of Bard College, Working Paper No. 66: 20.

Fetter, Frank Whitson. 1977. "Lenin, Keynes and Inflation." *Economica,* Vol. 44, No. 3 (February): 77–80.

Fine, B., K. O'Donnell and M. Prevezer. 1985. "Coal before Nationalisation." In B. Fine and L. Harris, eds. *The Peculiarities of the British Economy.* London: Lawrence and Wishart: 285–319.

Fisher, Irving. 1933. "The Debt Deflation Theory of Great Depressions." *Econometrica,* Vol. 1, No. 4 (October): 337–57.

Fletcher, W. 1904. *English and American Steam Carriages and Traction Engines.* Newton Abbot; reprinted David and Charles, 1973.

Flink, James J. 1975. *The Car Culture.* Cambridge: MIT Press.

Ford, Thomas. 1854. *History of Illinois.* Chicago: S. C. Griggs and Co.

Foreman-Peck, James. 1996. "Technological 'Lock-In' and the Power Source for the Motor Car." unpub. ms.

Foster, John Bellamy. 1997. "The Age of Planetary Crisis." *Review of Radical Political Economics,* Vol. 29, No. 4 (Fall): 113–42.

Freedman, Craig. 1998. "Countervailing Egos—Stigler Versus Galbraith." *History of Economics Review,* No. 27 (Winter): 50–75.

Freeman, Christopher, J. Clark, and L. Soete. 1982. *Unemployment and Technical Innovation: A Study of Long Waves and Economic Development.* London: Pinter.

Fresia, Jerry. 1988. *Toward an American Revolution: Exposing the Constitution and Other Illusions.* Boston: South End Press.

Frey, Bruno S., and Reiner Eichenberger. 1992. "Economics and Economists: A European Perspective." *American Economic Review,* Vol. 82, No. 2 (May): 216–20.

Frey, Bruno S., Werner W. Pomerehne, Friedrich Schneider, and Guy Gilbert. 1984. "Consensus and Dissension Among Economists: An Empirical Inquiry." *American Economic Review,* Vol. 74, No. 5 (December): 986–94.

Friedman, Milton. 1953a. "The Methodology of Positive." *Essays in Positive Economics.* Chicago: University of Chicago Press, 3–43.

———. 1953b. "The Case for Flexible Exchange Rates." *Essays in Positive Economics.* Chicago: University of Chicago Press: 157–203.

———. 1962. *Capitalism and Freedom.* Chicago: University of Chicago Press.

Friedman, Milton, and Anna Jacobson Schwartz. 1963. *A Monetary History of the United States, 1867–1960.* Princeton: Princeton University Press, 1971.

Froot, Kenneth, and J. Frankel. 1986. "Understanding the U.S. Dollar in the Eighties: The Expectations of Chartists and Fundamentalists," *Economic Record,* special issue (December): 24–38.

Froot, Kenneth A., and Richard H. Thaler. 1990. "Foreign Exchange." *Journal of Economic Perspectives,* Vol. 4, No. 3 (Summer): 179–92.

Furniss, Edgar Stephenson. 1920. *The Position of the Laborer in a System of Nationalism: A Study in the Labor Theories of the Later English Mercantilists.* New York: A. M. Kelley, 1965.

Galbraith, John Kenneth. 1967. *The New Industrial State.* Boston: Houghton Mifflin.

Georgescu-Roegen, Nicholas. 1990. "Thermodynamics, Economics, and Evolution." In Marcelo Alonso, ed., *Organization and Change in Complex Systems.* New York: Paragon House: 225–34.

Gerschenkron, A. 1962. "Economic Backwardness in Historical Perspective." In *Economic Backwardness in Historical Perspective: A Book of Essays.* Cambridge: Harvard University Press, 5–30.

Gertler, Mark, and Simon Gilchrist. 1994. "Monetary Policy, Business Cycles, and the Behavior of Small Manufacturing Firms." *Quarterly Journal of Economics,* Vol. 109, No. 2 (May): 309–40.

Gilbert, Martin. 1977. *Winston S. Churchill.* Vol. 5, *1922–1939: The Prophet of Truth.* Boston: Houghton Mifflin.

Goldschmidt, Richard Benedict. 1940. *The Material Basis of Evolution.* New Haven: Yale University Press.

Goode, Richard. 1994. "Gardiner Means on Administered Prices and Administrative Inflation." *Journal of Economic Issues,* Vol. 28, No. 1 (March): 173–86.

Gordon, David M., Richard Edwards, and Michael Reich. 1982. *Segmented Work, Divided Workers: The Historical Transformation of Labor in the United States.* Cambridge: Cambridge University Press.

Gordon, Robert J. 1988. "The Role of Wages in the Inflation Process." *American Economic Review,* Vol. 78, No. 2 (May): 276–83.

Gould, Stephen J. 1977a. "Evolution's Erratic Pace." *Natural History,* Vol. 86, No. 5 (May): 12–16.

———. 1977b. "The Return of Hopeful Monsters." *Natural History,* Vol. 86, No. 6 (June–July): 22–30.

———. 1989. *Wonderful Life: The Burgess Shale and the Nature of History.* New York: W. W. Norton.

———. 1993. *Eight Little Piggies: Reflections in Natural History.* New York: W. W. Norton.

———. 1994. "The Evolution of Life on the Earth." *Scientific American,* Vol. 271, No. 4 (October): 84–91.

———. 1996. *Full House: The Spread of Excellence from Plato to Darwin.* New York: Harmony Books.

Gowdy, John R. 1993. "Economic Selection and the Role of Government: Some Lessons from Evolutionary Biology." *Forum for Social Economics,* Vol. 22, No. 2 (Spring): 61–70.

Gramm, William P. 1972. "The Real Balance Effect in the Great Depression." *Journal of Economic History,* Vol. 32 (June–September): 499–519.

Greenwald, Bruce, and Joseph E. Stiglitz. 1993. "New and Old Keynesians." Journal of Economic Perspectives, Vol. 7, No. 1 (Winter): 23–44.

Habakkuk, H. J. 1962. *American and British Technology in the Nineteenth Century: The Search for Labour-Saving Inventions.* Cambridge: Cambridge University Press.

Hacker, Louis, M. 1940. *The Triumph of American Capitalism: The Development of Forces in American History to the End of the Nineteenth Century.* New York: Simon and Schuster.

Hagemann, Harald, and Michael Landesmann. 1997. "Lowe and Structural Theories of the Business Cycle." In Harald Hagemann and Heinz D. Kurz, eds., *Political Economics in Retrospect: Essays in Memory of Adolph Lowe.* Cheltenham: Edward Elgar, 95–130.

Halberstam, David. 1986. *The Reckoning.* New York: William Morrow.

Hammond, Bray. 1947. "Jackson, Biddle, and the Bank of the United States." *Journal of Economic History,* Vol. 7 (May): 1–23. Reprint. 1966. In Stanley Coben and Forest G. Hill, eds. *American Economic History: Essays in Interpretation.* Philadelphia: J. B. Lippincott, 224–44.

———. 1957. *Banks and Politics.* Princeton: University Press.

Handlin, Oscar, with Mary H. Handlin. 1945. "Origins of the American Business Corporation." *Journal of Economic History,* Vol. 5, No. 1 (May): 55–65.

Hannah, Leslie. 1998. "Survival and Size Mobility Among the World's Largest 100 Industrial Corporations." *American Economic Review: Papers and Proceedings,* Vol. 88, No. 2 (May): 62–5.

Hanssen, Andrew. 1998. "The Cost of Discrimination: A Study of Major League Baseball." *Southern Economic Journal,* Vol. 64, No. 3 (January): 603–27.

Harberger, Arnold C. 1954. "Monopoly and Resource Allocation." *American Economic Review: Proceedings,* Vol. 44 (May): 77–87.

———. 1998. "A Vision of the Growth Process." *American Economic Review,* Vol. 88, No. 1 (March): 1–32.

Hartz, Louis. 1948. *Economic Policy and Democratic Thought: Pennsylvania, 1776–1860.* Cambridge: Cambridge University Press.

Hawley, Ellis W. 1966. *The New Deal and the Problem of Monopoly.* Princeton: Princeton University Press.

Hawtrey, Ralph G. 1925. *The Economic Problem.* London: Longmans, Green.

Hayek, Friedrich A. 1941. *The Pure Theory of Capital.* Chicago: Midway Reprint, 1975.

Helleiner, Eric. 1994. *States and the Reemergence of Global Finance.* Ithaca: Cornell University Press.

Herodotus. 1942. *The Persian Wars,* George Rawlinson, trans. New York: Modern Library.

Hicks, John R. 1935. "Annual Survey of Economic Theory: The Theory of Monopoly." *Econometrica,* Vol. 3, No. 1 (January): 1–20.

Hirschman, Albert O. 1958. *The Strategy of Economic Development.* New Haven: Yale University Press.

———. 1971. *A Bias for Hope: Essays on Development and Latin America.* New Haven: Yale University Press.

———. 1981. "The Rise and Decline of Development Economics." *Essays in Trespassing: Economics to Politics and Beyond.* Cambridge: Cambridge University Press, 1–24.

Hopper, Gregory P. 1997. "What Determines the Exchange Rate: Economic Factors or Market Sentiment?" *Business Review of the Federal Reserve Bank of Philadelphia* (September-October): 17–29.

Houghton, John. 1693–1703. *A Collection for Improvement of Husbandry and Trade.* 4 vols. Reprint. 1969. Farnborough, Hants, England: Gregg International.

Hume, David. 1752. "Of Taxes." In T. H. Green and T. H. Grose, eds., *Essays: Moral, Political, and Literary.* Reprint. 1964. Aalen, Germany: Scientia Verlag, 356–60.

International Bank for Reconstruction and Development. 1996. *From Plan to Market: The World Development Report 1996.* New York: Oxford University Press.

Jackstadt, Stephen L., Lee Huskey, Don L. Marx, and Pershing J. Hill. 1990. "Economics 101 and an Economic Way of Thinking." *American Economist,* Vol. 34, No. 2 (Fall): 79–84.

Jaffe, Adam B., Steven R. Peterson, Paul R. Portney, and Robert N. Stavins. 1995. "Environmental Regulation and the Competitiveness of U.S. Manufacturing: What Does the Evidence Tell Us?" *Journal of Economic Literature,* Vol. 33, No. 1 (March): 132–63.

Jenks, Jeremiah. 1890. "The Economic Outlook." *Dial,* Vol. 10.

Jensen, Michael C. 1986. "Agency Costs of Free Cash Flow, Corporate Finance, and Takeovers." *American Economic Review,* Vol. 76, No. 2 (May): 323–9.

———. 1988. "Takeovers: Their Causes and Consequences." *Journal of Economic Perspectives,* Vol. 2, No. 1 (Winter): 21–48.

———. 1993. "The Modern Industrial Revolution: Exit and the Failure of Internal Control Systems." *Journal of Finance,* Vol. 48, No. 3 (July): 831–80.

Jensen, Michael, and William Meckling. 1976. "Theory of the Firm: Managerial Behavior, Agency Costs, and Ownership Structure." *Journal of Financial Economics,* Vol. 3: 305–60. Reprinted in part in Louis Putterman, ed., *The Economic Nature of the Firm: A Reader.* Cambridge: Cambridge University Press, 1986: 209–29.

Jensen, Michael, and Richard S. Ruback. 1983. "The Market for Corporate Control." *Journal of Financial Economics,* Vol. 11 (April): 5–50.

Jevons, William Stanley. 1865. *The Coal Question: An Enquiry Concerning the Progress of the Nation, and the Probable Exhaustion of Our Coal-Mines.* London: Macmillan.

———. 1879. "The Solar Influence on Commerce." In R. D. Collison Black and Rosamond Könekamp, eds. *Papers and Correspondence of William Stanley Jevons.* Vol. 7, *Papers on Political Economy.* London: Macmillan, 1972, 90–8.

———. 1882. "The Solar Commercial Cycle." *Nature,* 26 (6 July): 226–8; In R. D. Collison Black and Rosamond Könekamp, eds., *Papers and Correspondence of*

William Stanley Jevons, Vol. 7, *Papers on Political Economy.* London: Macmillan, 1972, 108–11.

Jung, Allen F. 1960. "Price Variations Among Automobile Dealers in Metropolitan Chicago." *Journal of Business,* Vol. 33 (January): 31–42.

Kagarlitsky, Boris. 1997. "The Russian Counterrevolution." *In These Times,* 14 April, 28–30.

Kaldor, Nicholas. 1939. "Speculation and Economic Stability." *Review of Economic Studies,* Vol. 7 (October): 1–27. Reprint In Nicholas Kaldor. 1960. *Essays on Economic Stability and Growth.* Glencoe, Ill.: Free Press, 17–39.

Kamien, Morton, and Nancy Schwartz. 1975. "Market Structure and Innovation: A Survey." *Journal of Economic Literature,* Vol. 13, No. 1 (March): 1–37.

Keynes, John Maynard. 1919. *The Economic Consequences of the Peace.* Vol. 2. *The Collected Writings of John Maynard Keynes.* London: Macmillan, 1972.

———. 1920–1926. "Keynes and Ancient Currencies." In Donald Moggridge, ed., *The Collected Writings of John Maynard Keynes.* Vol. 28, *Social, Political and Literary Writings.* London: Macmillan, 223–95.

———. 1923a. *A Tract on Monetary Reform.* Reprint as Donald Moggridge, ed., *The Collected Works of John Maynard Keynes,* vol. 4 London: Macmillan, 1971.

———. 1923b. "Currency Policy and Unemployment." *The Nation and Athenaeum* (11 August). Reprint in Donald Moggridge, ed., *The Collected Works of John Maynard Keynes,* Vol. 19, Pt. 1, 113–8.

———. 1924. "Alfred Marshall, 1842–1925." In *Essays in Biography.* Vol. 10, *The Collected Writings of John Maynard Keynes.* London: Macmillan, 1973, 161–231.

———. 1925. "The Economic Consequences of Mr. Winston Churchill." In Donald Maggridge, eds., *Essays in Persuasion.* Vol. 9, *The Collected Works of John Maynard Keynes,* London: Macmillan, 1972: 207–30.

———. 1926. "The End of Laissez-Faire." In *Essays in Persuasion,* Reprinted in Vol. 9, *The Collected Works of John Maynard Keynes.* London: Macmillan, 1972, 272–94.

———. 1930. *A Treatise on Money.* Vols. 5 and 6, *The Collected Writings of John Maynard Keynes,* ed. Donald Maggridge. London: Macmillan, 1971.

———. 1933. "The Means to Prosperity." In *Essays in Persuasion,* Vol. 9, *The Collected Works of John Maynard Keynes.* ed. Elizabeth Johnston. London: Macmillan, 1972, 335–66.

———. 1936. *The General Theory of Employment, Interest and Money.* New York: Macmillan.

———. 1938. "The Policy of Government Storage of Food Stuffs and Raw Materials." *Economic Journal,* Vol. 191, No. 48 (September): 449–460. Reprint in *The Collected Writings of John Maynard Keynes.* Vol. 31, 456–70.

Kindleberger, Charles P. 1961. "Obsolescence and Technical Change." *Bulletin of the Oxford University Institute of Statistics,* Vol. 23, No. 3 (August): 281–97.

Klein, B. H. 1977. *Dynamic Economics.* Cambridge: Harvard University Press.

Klein, Judy L. 1997. *Statistical Visions in Time: A History of Time Series Analysis, 1662–1938.* Cambridge: Cambridge University Press.

Klepper, Stephen, and Kenneth L. Simons. 1997. "Technological Extinctions of Industrial Firms: An Inquiry Into Their Nature and Causes." *Industrial and Corporate Change,* Vol. 6, No. 2 (March): 379–460.

Kolko, Gabriel. 1963. *The Triumph of Conservatism.* New York: Free Press.

———. 1965. *Railroads and Regulation, 1877–1916.* Princeton: Princeton University Press.

Koopmans, Tjalling. 1947. "Measurement without Theory." *Review of Economics and Statistics,* Vol. 29: 157–81.

Kroos, Herman E., and Charles Gilbert. 1972. *American Business History.* Englewood Cliffs, N.J.: Prentice-Hall.

Krugman, Paul R. 1989. *Exchange Rate Instability: The Lionel Robbins Lectures.* Cambridge: MIT Press.

———. 1990. *Rethinking International Trade.* Cambridge: MIT Press.

———. 1997. "Currency Crises." Paper prepared for National Bureau of Economic Research Conference on International Capital Flows, Woodstock, Vermont, October 17–18.

Kuhn, Thomas S. 1962. *The Structure of Scientific Revolutions.* Chicago: University of Chicago Press.

Kuznets, Simon. 1930a. "Equilibrium Economics and Business Cycle Theory." *Quarterly Journal of Economics,* Vol. 44 (May): 381–415.

———. 1930b. *Secular Movements in Production and Prices: Their Nature and their Bearing upon Cyclical Fluctuations.* New York: A. M. Kelley, 1967.

———. 1940. "Schumpeter's *Business Cycles.*" *American Economic Review,* Vol. 30 (June): 57–71. Reprinted in his *Economic Change: Selected Essays in Business Cycles, National Income and Economic Growth.* New York: W. W. Norton, 1954: 105–24.

———. 1947. "Economic Trends and Business Cycles." In his *Economic Change: Selected Essays in Business Cycles, National Income and Economic Growth.* New York: W. W. Norton, 1954, 125–44.

Lamoreaux, Naomi. 1985. *The Great Merger Movement in American Business, 1895–1904.* New York: Cambridge University Press.

Lancaster, Kelvin, and R. G. Lipsey. 1956. "The General Theory of the Second Best." *Review of Economic Studies,* Vol. 24, No. 1 (January): 11–32.

Leakey, Richard, and Roger Lewin. 1995. *The Sixth Extinction.* New York: Doubleday: 44–56.

Lee, Frederic S. 1984. "The Marginalist Controversy and the Demise of Full Cost Pricing." *Journal of Economic Issues,* Vol. 18, No. 4 (December): 1107–31.

Leibenstein, Harvey. 1966. "Allocative Efficiency and X-Efficiency." *American Economic Review,* Vol. 56, 392–415. Reprinted in Louis Putterman, ed. *The Economic Nature of the Firm: A Reader.* Cambridge: Cambridge University Press, 1986, 165–9.

———. 1978a. "X-inefficiency Xists—Reply to an Xorcist." *American Economic Review,* Vol. 68, No. 1 (March): 203–11.

———. 1978b. "On the Basic Proposition of X-Efficiency Theory." *American Economic Review Papers and Proceedings,* Vol. 68, No. 2 (May): 328–32.

Levine, A. L. 1967. *Industrial Retardation in Britain, 1880–1914.* New York: Basic Books.

Levine, David. 1992. "Can Wage Increases Pay for Themselves? Tests with a Production Function." *Economic Journal,* Vol. 102, No. 414 (September): 1102–16.

Liebowitz, S. J., and Stephen E. Margolis. 1995. "Path Dependence, Lock-in and History." *Journal of Law, Economics and Organization,* Vol. 11, No. 1 (April): 205–26.

Livingston, James. 1986. *Origins of the Federal Reserve System: Money, Class, and Corporate Capitalism, 1890–1913.* Ithaca: Cornell University Press.

———. 1994. *Pragmatism and the Political Economy of Cultural Revolution, 1850–1940.* Chapel Hill: University of North Carolina Press.

Louca, Francisco. 1997. *Turbulence in Economics: An Evolutionary Appraisal of Cycles and Complexity in Historical Processes.* Cheltenham: Edward Elgar.

McCraw, Thomas K., and Forest Reinhardt. 1989. "Losing to Win: U.S. Steel's Pricing, Investment Decisions, and Market Share, 1901–1938." *Journal of Economic History,* Vol. 49, No. 3 (September): 593–619.

McLaughlin, Charles C. 1967. "The Stanley Steamer: Study in Unsuccessful Innovation." In Hugh G. J. Aitken, ed., *Explorations in Enterprise.* Cambridge: Harvard University Press, 259–72.

Mager, Nathan H. 1987. *The Kondratieff Wave.* New York: Praeger.

Mandel, Ernest. 1970. *Marxian Economic Theory.* 2 vols. New York: Monthly Review Press.

Marris, Robin. 1964. *The Economic Theory of Managerial Capitalism.* Glencoe, Ill.: Free Press.

Marshall, Alfred. 1890. *Principles of Economics: An Introductory Volume.* London: Macmillan.

Marx, Karl. 1963–1971. *Theories of Surplus Value,* 3 Parts (Moscow: Progress Publishers).

Marx, Karl. 1849–51. *Londoner Hefte.* In Karl Marx and Friedrich Engels, *Gesamtausgabe.* Vierte Abteilung. Band 7. *Exzerpte und Notizen, September 1849 bis Febuar 1851.* Berlin: Dietz, 1983.

———. 1967. *Capital.* 3 vols. New York: International Publishers.

———. 1977. *Capital.* Vol. 1. New York: Vintage.

———and Frederick Engels. 1848. *Communist Manifesto.* In Karl Marx and Frederick Engels, *Selected Works in Three Volumes.* New York: International Publishers, 1970, i: 98–141.

———. 1973. *Marx-Engels Werke.* Berlin: Dietz Verlag.

Mayhew, Anne. 1990. "The Sherman Act as Protective Reaction." *Journal of Economic Issues,* Vol. 24, No. 2 (June): 389–96.

Means, Gardiner C. 1975. "Simultaneous Inflation and Unemployment: A Challenge to Theory and Policy." *Challenge,* Vol. 18, No. 4 (September/October):

6–20. Reprinted in Gardiner Means et al. 1975. *The Roots of Inflation: The International Crisis.* New York: Burt Franklin: 1–33.

Mehra, Yash P. 1991. "Wage Growth and the Inflation Process: An Empirical Note." *American Economic Review,* Vol. 81, No. 4 (September): 931–37.

Mill, John Stuart. 1848. *Principles of Political Economy with Some of Their Applications to Social Philosophy.* Vols. 2–3, *Collected Works.* J. M. Robson, ed. Toronto: University of Toronto Press, 1965.

Mirowski, Philip. 1984. "Macroeconomic Instability and the 'Natural' Processes in Early Neoclassical Economics." *Journal of Economic History,* Vol. 44, No. 2 (June): 345–54. Reprinted in Philip Mirowski. 1988. *Against Mechanism: Protecting Economics from Science.* Totowa, N.J.: Rowman and Littlefield: 45–56.

———. ed. 1994. *Natural Images in Economic Thought: Markets Read in Tooth and Claw.* Cambridge: Cambridge University Press.

———. 1988. "Problems of Paternity of Econometrics: Henry Ludwell Moore." *History of Political Economy,* Vol. 22, No. 4 (Winter): 587–609.

Mishkin, F. S. 1977. "What Depressed the Consumer? The Household Balance Sheet and the 1973–1975 Recession." *Brookings Papers on Economic Activity,* No. 1: 123–64.

———. 1978. "The Household Balance Sheet and the Great Depression." *Journal of Economic History,* Vol. 38, No. 4 (December): 918–37.

Mitchell, Wesley Clare. 1913. *Business Cycles.* New York: Burt Franklin, 1970.

Moggridge, Donald Edward. 1969. *The Return to Gold, 1925: The Formulation of Economic Policy and its Critics.* London: Cambridge University Press.

Mokyr, Joel. 1990a. "Punctuated Equilibria and Technological Progress." *American Economic Review,* Vol. 80, No. 2 (May): 350–54.

Mokyr, Joel. 1990b. *The Lever of Riches: Technological Creativity and Economic Progress.* New York: Oxford University Press.

Morgenstern, Oskar. 1963. *On the Accuracy of Economic Observations.* 2d ed. Princeton: Princeton University Press.

Morris, Simon Conway. 1995. "A New Phylum from the Lobster's Lips." *Nature,* 14 December, 661.

National Resources Committee. 1939. *The Structure of the American Economy.* Washington, D.C.: National Resources Committee.

Nelson, Richard and Sidney Winter. 1982. *An Evolutionary Theory of Economic Change.* Cambridge, Mass: Belknap Press.

Nickell, Stephen, Daphne Nicolitsas, and Neil Dryden. 1997. "What Makes Firms Perform Well?" *European Economic Review,* Vol. 41, Nos. 3–5: 507–16.

Nurkse, Ragnar. 1944. *International Currency Experience.* Geneva: League of Nations.

O'Donnell, Rod. 1992. "The Unwritten Books and Papers of J. M. Keynes." *History of Political Economy,* Vol. 24, No. 4 (Winter): 767–817.

Oppenheim, A. L. 1957. "A Bird's Eye View of Mesopotamian Economic History." In Karl Polanyi, Conrad M. Arensberg, and Harry W. Pearson, eds. *Trade and Market in the Early Empires.* Glencoe, Ill.: Free Press, 27–37.

Palley, Thomas I. 1997. "Does Inflation Grease the Wheels of Adjustment? New Evidence from the U.S. Economy." *International Review of Applied Economics,* Vol. 11, No. 3 (January): 387–98.

———. 1998. *Plenty of Nothing: The Downsizing of the American Dream and the Case for Structural Keynesianism.* Princeton: Princeton University Press.

Papadimitriou, Dimitri B., and L. Randall Wray. 1997. "The Institutional Prerequisites for Successful Capitalism." *Journal of Economic Issues,* Vol. 31, No. 2 (June): 493–500.

Patnaik, Prabhat. 1997. Accumulation and Stability under Capitalism. Oxford: Claredon Press.

Peart, Sandra J. 1991. "Sunspots and Expectations: W. S. Jevons' Theory of Economic Fluctuations." *Journal of the History of Economic Thought,* Vol. 13, No. 2 (Fall): 343–65.

Perelman, Michael. 1977. *Farming for Profit in a Hungry World: Capital and the Crisis in Agriculture.* Totowa, N.J.: Allenhald, Osmun.

———. 1993. *The Pathology of the U.S. Economy: The Costs of a Low Wage System.* New York: St. Martin's.

———. 1996. *The End of Economics.* London: Routledge.

Peritz, Rudolph J. R. 1996. *Competition Policy in America, 1888–1992.* New York: Oxford University Press.

Peyton, John L. 1869. *Over the Alleghenies.* Extracted in Warren S. Tryon, ed. 1952. *A Mirror for Americans,* 3 vols. Chicago: University of Chicago Press: Vol. 3: 589–607.

Phillips, G. A. 1976. *General Strike: The Politics of Industrial Conflict.* London: Weidenfeld and Nicolson.

Piore, Michael J. 1968. "The Impact of the Labor Market upon the Design and Selection of Productive Techniques within the Manufacturing Plant." *Quarterly Journal of Economics,* Vol. 82, No. 4 (November): 602–20.

Polanyi, Karl. 1944. *The Great Transformation: The Political Origins of Our Time.* Boston: Beacon Press.

———. 1957. "Marketless Trading in Hammurabi's Time." In Karl Polanyi, Conrad M. Arensberg, and Harry W. Pearson, eds., *Trade and Market in the Early Empires.* Glencoe, Ill.: Free Press, 12–26.

Pool, Robert. 1989. "Strange Bedfellows." *Science,* 18 August, 700–705.

Porter, Michael E. 1990. *The Competitive Advantage of Nations.* New York: Free Press.

Porter, Michael E., and Claas van der Linde. 1995a. "Green and Competitive: Ending the Stalemate." *Harvard Business Review,* Vol. 73, No. 5 (September-October): 120–34.

———. 1995b. "Toward a New Conception of the Environment-Competitiveness Relationship." *Journal of Economic Perspectives,* Vol. 9, No. 4 (Fall): 97–118.

Quigley, Carroll. 1966. *Tragedy and Hope: A History of the World in Our Time.* New York: Macmillan.

Reder, Melvin W. 1982. "Chicago Economics: Permanence and Change." *Journal of Economic Literature,* Vol. 20, No. 1 (March): 1–38.

Reuff, Jacques. 1964. *The Age of Inflation*. Chicago: Regnery.

Ricardo, David, 1817. *Principles of Political Economy.* Vol. 1 of Piero Sraffa and Maurice Dobb, eds., *The Works and Correspondence of David Ricardo.* 11 vols. Cambridge: Cambridge University Press, 1951–73.

Robbins. Lionel. 1935. *The Great Depression*. London: Macmillan.

Robertson, Dennis. 1928. *Money.* New York: Pitman.

Roney, H. B. 1907. "Efforts to Check the Slaughter." In W. B. Mershon, ed., *The Passenger Pigeon.* New York: Outing Publishing Company.

Rosenberg, Alexander. 1994. "Does Evolutionary Theory Give Comfort or Inspiration to Economics?" In Philip Mirowski, ed., *Natural Images in Economic Thought: Markets Read in Tooth and Claw.* Cambridge: Cambridge University Press.

Rosenberg, Nathan. 1969. "The Direction of Technological Change: Inducement Mechanism and Focusing Devices." *Economic Development and Cultural Change.* Reprinted in *Perspectives on Technology.* Cambridge: Cambridge University Press, 1976, 108–25.

Samuelson, Paul Anthony. 1955. *Economics: An Introductory Analysis.* 3d ed. New York: McGraw-Hill.

Scherer, F. M., and David Ross. 1990. *Industrial Market Structure and Economic Performance.* 3d ed. Boston: Houghton Mifflin.

Schoenhof, Jacob. 1893. *The Economy of High Wages: An Inquiry into the Cause of High Wages and Their Effects on Methods and Cost of Production.* New York: G. P. Putnam's Sons.

Schumpeter, Joseph Alois. 1934. "Depressions." In Douglas V. Brown, ed., *The Economics of the Recovery Program.* New York: McGraw-Hill: 3–21.

———. 1935. "The Analysis of Economic Change." *Review of Economic Statistics,* Vol. 17, No. 4 (May): 2–10.

———. 1939. *Business Cycles: A Theoretical, Historical and Statistical Analysis of the Capitalist Process,* 2 vols. New York: McGraw-Hill.

———. 1941. "The Economic Interpretation of Our Time: The Lowell Lectures." In Richard Swedberg, ed., *The Economics and Sociology of Capitalism.* Princeton: Princeton University Press, 1991, 339–400.

———. 1943. "Capitalism in the Postwar World." In R. Clemence, ed. *Essays of Joseph Schumpeter.* Cambridge, Mass.: Addison Wesley, 1951, 170–83.

———. 1950. *Capitalism, Socialism and Democracy,* 3d. ed. New York: Harper and Row.

———. 1954. *History of Economic Analysis.* New York: Oxford University Press.

———. 1961. *The Theory of Economic Development: An Inquiry into Profits, Capital, Credit, Interest, and the Business Cycle.* Cambridge: Harvard University Press.

Schweickart, David. 1996. *Against Capitalism.* Boulder, Colo.: Westview Press.

Sent, E.-M. 1997. "Sargent versus Simon: Bounded Rationality Unbound." *Cambridge Journal of Economics,* Vol. 21, No. 3 (May): 323–38.

Sherman, Howard J. 1983. "Cyclical Behavior of Government Fiscal Policy." *Journal of Economic Issues,* Vol. 17, No. 2 (June): 379–88.

———. 1991. *The Business Cycle: Growth and Crisis under Capitalism.* Princeton: Princeton University Press.

Shleifer, Andrei, and Lawrence H. Summers. 1988. "Breach of Trust in Hostile Takeovers." In Alan J. Auerbach, ed., *Corporate Takeovers: Causes and Consequences.* Chicago: University of Chicago Press, 33–61.

Silk, Leonard Solomon, and Mark Silk. 1996. *Making Capitalism Work.* New York: New York University Press.

Simon, Herbert Alexander. 1979. "Rational Decision Making in Business Organizations." *American Economic Review,* Vol. 69, No 4 (September): 493–513.

———. 1996. *The Sciences of the Artificial,* 3d ed. Cambridge: MIT Press.

Simons, Algie Martin. 1925. *Social Forces in American History.* New York: Macmillan.

Skidelsky, Robert. 1992. *John Maynard Keynes.* Vol. 2. *The Economist as Savior, 1920–1937.* London: Macmillan.

Sloan, Alfred Pritchard. 1964. *My Years with General Motors.* Garden City, N.Y.: Doubleday.

Slutsky, Eugen. 1937. "The Summation of Random Causes as the Source of Cyclic Processes." *Econometrica,* Vol. 5, 105–45.

Smith, Adam. 1759. *The Theory of Moral Sentiments,* D. D. Raphael and A. L. Macfie, eds. (Oxford: Clarendon Press, 1976).

———. 1776. *The Nature and Causes of the Wealth of Nations.* Oxford: Oxford University Press, 1976.

Sowell, Thomas. 1993. "A Student's Eye View of George Stigler." *Journal of Political Economy,* Vol. 101, No. 5, 784–93.

Sraffa, Piero. 1926. "The Laws of Returns under Competitive Conditions." *Economic Journal* (December): 535–50.

Stanners, W. 1996. "Inflation and Growth." *Cambridge Journal of Economics,* Vol. 20, No. 4 (July): 509–12.

Stein, Herbert. 1991. "What Economic Advisers Do." *American Enterprise* (March/April): 6–12.

Stevens, William K. 1998. "Plant Survey Reveals Many Species Threatened with Extinction." *New York Times,* 9 April.

Stigler, George J. 1961. "The Economics of Information." *Journal of Political Economy,* Vol. 69, No. 3 (June): 213–25.

———. 1968. "The Dominant Firm and the Inverted Umbrella." In *The Organization of Industry.* Homewood, Ill.: Richard D. Irwin.

———. 1976. "The Xistence of X-Efficiency." *American Economic Review,* Vol. 66, No. 1 (March): 213–36.

Stiglitz, Joseph. 1981. "Potential Competition May Reduce Welfare." *American Economic Review,* Vol. 71, No. 2 (May): 184–9.

Stolper, Wolfgang. 1994. *Joseph Alois Schumpeter: The Public Life of a Private Man.* Princeton: Princeton University Press.

Stonebraker, Robert J. 1979. "Turnover and Mobility among the 100 Largest Firms: An Update." *American Economic Review,* Vol. 69, No. 5 (December): 968–73.

Strassman, W. P. 1959. *Risk and Technological Investment.* Ithaca: Cornell University Press.

Streeck, Wolfgang. 1992. *Social Institutions and Economic Performance: Studies of Industrial in Advanced Capitalist Economies.* New York: Sage.

———. 1997. "Beneficial Constraints: On the Economic Limits of Rational Voluntarism." In J. Rogers Hollingsworth and Robert Boyer, eds. *Contemporary Capitalism: The Embeddedness of Institutions.* Cambridge: Cambridge University Press: 197–219.

Sullivan, Allanna. 1990. "Stretched Thin: Exxon's Restructuring in the Past Is Blamed for Recent Accidents." *Wall Street Journal,* 16 March, A1, A14.

Suzumura, Kotaro. 1995. *Competition, Commitment, and Welfare.* Oxford: Clarendon Press.

Suzumura, K., and K. Kiyono. 1987. "Entry Barriers and Economic Welfare." *Review of Economic Studies,* Vol. 54, No. 1 (January): 157–67.

Sweezy, Paul M. 1954. Review of J. Steindl, *Maturity and Stagnation in American Capitalism. Econometrica,* Vol. 22, No. 4 (October): 531–3.

Sylos-Labini, Paolo. 1982. "Rigid Prices, Flexible Prices and Inflation." *Banca Nazionale Del Lavoro Quarterly Review,* No. 140 (March): 37–68. Reprinted in his *The Forces of Growth and Decline.* Cambridge: MIT Press, 1984: 147–82.

Telser, Lester. 1987. *A Theory of Efficient Cooperation and Competition.* Cambridge: Cambridge University Press.

Temin, Peter. 1969. *The Jacksonian Economy.* New York: Norton.

———. 1989. *Lessons from the Great Depression: The Lionel Robbins Lectures for 1989.* Cambridge: MIT Press.

Thurow, Lester C. 1992. *Head to Head: The Coming Economic Battle among Japan, Europe and America.* New York: William Morrow.

Tober, James Allen. 1973. "The Allocation of Wildlife Resources in the United States, 1850–1900." Ph. D. dissertation, Department of Economics, Yale University.

———. 1981. *Who Owns the Wildlife?: The Political Economy of Conservation in Nineteenth-Century America.* Westport, Conn.: Greenwood Press.

Tobin, James. 1974. *The New Economics One Decade Older: The Eliot Janeway Lectures on Historical Economics in Honor of Schumpeter, 1972.* Princeton: Princeton University Press.

———. 1978. "A Proposal for International Monetary Reform." *Eastern Economic Journal,* Vol. 4, Nos. 3–4 (July/October): 153–9.

———. 1980. *Asset Accumulation and Economic Activity: Reflections on Contemporary Economic Macroeconomic Theory.* Chicago: University of Chicago Press.

Tocqueville, Alexis de. 1848. *Democracy in America,* trans. Henry Reeve. 2 vols. New York: D. Appleton, 1899.

Tolstoy, Leo, 1970. *Anna Karenina.* New York: W. W. Norton.

Trotsky, Leon. 1932. *The Russian Revolution: The Overthrow of Tzarism and the Triumph of the Soviets,* ed., F. W. Dupee, New York: Doubleday.

Tsuru, Shigeto. 1993. *Japan's Capitalism: Creative Defeat and Beyond*. Cambridge: Cambridge University Press.

Turner, Jonathan H. 1985. *Herbert Spencer: A Renewed Appreciation*. Beverly Hills: Sage Publications.

Uchitelle, Louis. 1998. "The Accidental Inventor of Today's Capitalism." *New York Times,* 21 February, B 7.

Utterback, J. M., and F. F. Suarez. 1993. "Innovation, Competition, and Industry Structure." *Research Policy,* Vol. 15: 285–305.

U. S. Department of Commerce, Bureau of the Census. 1975. *Historical Statistics of the United States: Colonial Times to 1970*. Washington, D.C.: U.S.G.P.O.

Vanek, Jaroslav. 1989. *Crisis and Reform: East and West*. Ithaca: Author.

Veblen, Thorstein. 1915. *Imperial Germany and the Industrial Revolution*. New York: Macmillan.

———. 1921. *The Engineers and the Price System*. New York: Viking Press, 1938. Reprint. 1965. New York: A. M. Kelley.

Vickers, J. 1995. "Concepts of Competition." *Oxford Economic Papers,* Vol. 47, No. 1 (January): 1–23.

Walras, Leon. 1874. *Elements of Pure Economics, or The Theory of Social Wealth,* trans. William Jaffe. Homewood, Ill.: Richard D. Irwin, 1954.

Ward, Mark. 1998. "Wired for Mayhem." *New Scientist,* 4 July, 7.

Welles, Chris. 1990. "Exxon's Future: What Has Larry Rawl Wrought." *Business Week,* 2 April, 72–6.

Wells, David A. 1889. *Recent Economic Changes, And Their Effect on the Production and Well-Being of Society.* New York: Da Capo Press, 1970.

Whaples, Robert. 1995. "Where Is There Consensus among American Economic Historians?" *Journal of Economic History,* Vol. 55, No. 1 (March): 139–54.

Wilson, Edward O. 1992. *The Diversity of Life.* Cambridge: Harvard University Press.

Wood, Adrian. 1995. "How Trade Hurt Unskilled Workers." *Journal of Economic Perspectives,* Vol. 9, No. 3 (Summer): 57–80.

Wright, Gavin. 1990. "The Origins of American Industrial Success, 1870–1940." *American Economic Review,* Vol. 80, No. 4 (September): 651–68.

Index